Errata:

Page 69, 5th line from bottom:
I was no longer a POW
but still an Italian soldier,
stationed in Livorno, at that time.

Page 74, paragraph 2, 4th line:
date should be January **1946.**

Page 76, line 3 from bottom:
date should be July 5, **1946.**

CASA MIRALAGO

The Autobiography of Hugo Redivo

Casa Miralago

An Okanagan Photographer's Journey
1919 - 1961

[signature: Hugo Redivo]

LAKESIDE
PUBLISHING
Penticton, British Columbia
2006

ISBN 0-9739466-3-6

LIBRARY AND ARCHIVES CANADA CATALOGUING IN PUBLICATION
Redivo, Hugo
Casa Miralago : an Okanagan photographer's journey / Hugo Redivo.
ISBN 0-9739466-3-6
1. Redivo, Hugo.
2. Photographers – British Columbia – Okanagan Valley (Region) – Biography.
I. Title.
TR140.R426A3 2006   770'.92   C2006-907107-9

The photographs in this book are included for their historical value
more than their photographic merit.

Front cover photograph by Ole Westby

Edited by Harold Rhenisch
Chapters 13 and 17 by Dorothy Vögeli translated by Harold Rhenisch

Produced in association with Okanagan Bookworks
http://www.booksokanagan.com

Lakeside Publishing
4529 Lakeside Road, Penticton BC V2A 8W4
http://www.redivo-photoart.com

Table of Contents

1. Only a Labourer

I was born on July 28, 1919 in Wiesbaden, Germany, to an Italian father, Domenico Pasquale Redivo, and a German mother, Elsa Portner. It was eight-and-a-half months after the armistice of World War I. The war had lasted over four years and had taken its toll on the family.

When war broke out in August 1914, my parents had two small children, four and five years old: my brother Bruno and my sister Lola. Because my father was an Italian citizen, he became an enemy alien when Italy declared war on Germany in 1915, and was required to report daily to the authorities. Luckily, as he had a German wife and children, he was not interned, and could continue to provide for his family. His work as an independent terrazzo and cement contractor took him into the surrounding countryside, which made it difficult for him to report regularly to the police. In time, though, he became so well known and trusted at the police station that my mother was accepted as a substitute and made his reports for him. This arrangement allowed him to stay overnight in distant places deep in the farming country and to complete his jobs without having to return nightly to the city.

My father was well respected by the villagers for his skill at laying terrazzo floors, and for producing terrazzo steps for staircases, gravestones, kitchen sinks and windowsills. Terrazzo is a cement combination, with small black, white or red granite stones, or white and red together, which have a beautiful, smooth, decorative finish after being polished with a grinding stone. Sometimes mosaic designs are included in floors. To the people who did not know him well, my father was "just an Italian," but because he had his own business he was not considered "only a labourer."

Working for farmers out in the countryside was a great advantage. My father was able to eat freely and could bring home fresh farm food – eggs, meats and produce. As food was heavily rationed during the entire war, however, that was a very risky undertaking and was considered *hamstern*, hoarding. As the war years went on, without peace in sight, and as rations became smaller and smaller, the food from the countryside became more and more important. Unfortunately, whenever my father was caught bringing food home it was confiscated and his family went hungry again.

During the years of war, my mother lost four members of her immediate family: the flu epidemic that ravaged all of Europe in the year following the war took her mother, a paralyzed aunt who lived in the same house, and her sister, while tuberculosis, a consequence of malnutrition, took my sister Lola in May 1918. Despite my birth fifteen months later, my mother never fully recovered from that loss. I believe that she wished I had been a girl as a comforting replacement for my lost sister.

When I was born, the family still lived in Wiesbaden. My father was forty-four years old. My mother was thirty-eight. Before World War I, Wiesbaden was the summer residence of the European aristocracy, especially of the Emperor of Germany and the Tsar of Russia. The Tsarina was a German princess. A Russian Orthodox chapel, its domes adorned with gold, which served the Russian Tsar and his entourage, still stands overlooking the city from the top of the Neroberg. The entire family was executed in 1917, during the Bolshevik Revolution. As the name implies, Wiesbaden is a spa, with therapeutic waters, fine cultural venues like the Staatstheater, and the Kurhaus with its casino. It was the playground of the European nobility and the high society of the times. During the Second World War, the Allies dropped leaflets over the city that read, Wicsbaden werden wir schonen, denn dort wollen wir wohnen. It was a rhyming slogan meaning, "Wiesbaden we will spare because we want to live there." And, truly, hardly any bombs were dropped on the city. Of course, there was no war industry.

Even in 1919, the year of my birth, food was still very scarce in Wiesbaden, and still strictly rationed, as the continuing British blockade allowed little food, if any, to enter Germany. My parents decided to move into the countryside, where the farmers had enough food to eat and even to sell, and where most of my father's jobs were. They made the move with regret, but the family's survival was imperative. We made the move in February 1921, when I was one-and-a-half, and settled in Dalheim in Rheinhessen, a farming village of about seven hundred souls, thirty-five kilometres south of Wiesbaden. Dalheim is centred in a mixed-farming and wine-growing region six kilometres from where the Rhine flows past the famous wine town of Nierstein, and near the equally famous wine city of Oppenheim. Because Nierstein and Oppenheim are significant wine-growing centres, they contain many old wine cellars. In some years, in some locations, groundwater enters these cellars during harvest time. My father chose to settle in Dalheim because he was an expert at waterproofing such cellars.

It may be hard to believe that an eighteen-month-old child would have any memories of that time, but I do. Because of our move, I was left with neighbours in the house in Wiesbaden. I remember the lady, Frau Wintermeyer, and her daughter Else. I stayed with them for about a week until the move to Dalheim was completed and my parents had settled into an old house there. This house was the only accommodation available in the village at that time, and we lived in it from 1921 until 1925, when we moved into a new house my father built himself. That first house was at least two hundred years old. It was built of clay and straw blocks, had a very small kitchen, one small bedroom, a tiny upstairs attic room, and a living room (only slightly bigger), all with very low ceilings. There was no running water, no electricity, and no indoor toilet. The windows were small and the front door was divided, like you would find in a stable. Nothing was level or square. The old house was situated at the edge of the village's open wastewater gutter. The rooms were always damp.

Caring for the family under these conditions gave my mother some very hard years, but at least we had enough to eat. This was especially important to our family, since my parents had moved to the village so that I would have enough fresh milk and would not die of malnutrition, as had my sister.

In Dalheim my mother had to cope with many conditions to which she was not accustomed. The first shock was the language. Coming from the city, she was used to speaking High German, but in the village the people spoke a very coarse and at times rude dialect that she could not understand. Apart from the many misunderstandings, she was often teased because along with the two schoolteachers and the parson she and her family were the only ones in the village who spoke differently. One of her first surprises was hearing shouting outside, amongst which she made out obscenities attached to the names Bruno and Hugo. She could not understand why someone would shout like that at her children! It turned out that the neighbours' dogs had the same names as my brother and me, and their owners were shouting at them in that crude village dialect.

My mother had to carry the family's daily two buckets of water home from a fountain about a hundred meters from the house. Most houses in the village had running water and electricity by that time, but a few still did not. Ours was one of those. I can still see my brother doing his homework under candlelight. The light was somewhat better in the kitchen and living room, where a larger coal oil lamp attached to the wall cast an overall glow.

The house was unhealthy, too. I remember being very sick for a long time, but do not know from what. I know I was in bed for months on end, because when I was allowed to get up from bed I had to learn to walk again, even though I was already about three years old. I was told my sickness was partly because the house was so cold, damp and draughty. We were saved from it when my mother's cousin, Edward Schutt, came to visit from Copenhagen. Because Denmark was not in that so-called "Great War," "the war to end all wars," he had hard currency, which was worth a lot in post-war Germany, where galloping inflation was in progress. When he saw the conditions in which his cousin had to live, and what she had to endure to raise her family, he decided to help her out. As a retired movie house owner he had some spare money, some of which he made available to my mother so that my father could start building a new house. In the spring of 1925, we moved in.

That is the year I started school. Of my school years I have mixed memories: some good, some bad. For one thing, because I was sick I did not start with the others the first day of school. As a result, when I started school a week or two later I was already marked as an outsider. What's more, because I spoke High German, as did my mother, I appeared odd to them and was teased continually. Teasing and further abuse came my way because of how my mother dressed me, that's to say in good "city" clothes, with a neat little overcoat, which my school chums called Scheissmäntelchen (shitty little coat). Adding to this odd situation was the way I was welcomed by the teacher, Fräulein Schauss, who came from the city of Darmstadt. Even though I only had Fräulein Schauss for one year, I have never forgotten her. On my first visit back to Europe in 1959, after ten years in Canada, I passed through Darmstadt. Remembering her, I told the gas station attendant that my teacher in grade one was from Darmstadt, and that I remembered that her name was Fräulein Schauss. He stopped filling my tank and said, "That is my aunt!" We both were very surprised, but, sadly, she was not alive any more.

Because I spoke so well and was so cutely dressed, Miss Schauss welcomed me by bending over and hugging me profusely in front of the whole class. I believe that is the first time that I was consciously aware of the softness and the charming existence of a woman's bosom. The whole class of about forty children, consisting of grades one to four in that one room, witnessed Miss Schauss singling me out. That sense of difference stayed with me throughout my eight years in that school. To top it all off, I did not have a German name like Schmidt, Baum, or Müller, but Redivo – the only foreign name in the entire countryside. Immediately, my name was distorted into Radedsky, Razzi, Terrazzi and many other variations – and because the name is Italian they came up with derogatory descriptions for Italians like *Mausfallenkrämer* (mouse trap dealer) and *Dreibund Veräter* (traitor of the Triple Alliance, the pact of 1882 between Germany, Austria-Hungary and Italy).

Another way in which I stood out was the fact that I always had good grades and a good report card. This was not always to my advantage in dealing with my "friends." I recall one test that was given to the grade seven class while I was, once again, sick at home in bed. It was a surprise history test and the teacher forbade the students to tell me about it. Dutifully, no one told me anything, and when I showed up back in class, the teacher, Karl Brenner (who had also come from Darmstadt), put me on a side table and gave me a list with thirty historical dates from the years 9 through 1918. Within the time limit of the test, I had to name the events that happened on those dates. I answered twenty-nine dates correctly – no one else was even close to this result. The grades given at that time went from 1 (very good) to 5 (insufficient). The teacher asked the class if he should give me a 1, or a 1-2. I got a 1-2. The girls all shouted, "Give him a 1!" but the boys voted for giving me the lesser mark.

History caused further problems. I was beaten up when the teacher dealt with the topic of the 1914-1918 war. Before that war, Italy was in the *Dreiländer Bund* (the Triple Alliance) with Germany and Austria. Designed by Bismarck, who was the German Chancellor at the time, the purpose of the pact was to prevent Italy from attacking Austria at any time and to prevent Italy from remaining neutral if its pact partners should ever be in a war. One of the conditions of the pact was that the partners would consult with each other if they entered a war with another nation. There was also a codicil that Italy would not adhere to pact conditions if England were to be involved in a war. At the opening of the 1914-1918 war, and contrary to the terms of the Alliance, Austria and Germany did not consult Italy. In the beginning, when Austria declared war on Serbia in August 1914 and the whole conflagration started, many of the central European powers declared war on each other. Italy remained neutral. Eventually, however, in 1915, she entered the war against her former pact partners. That's why I was beaten.

A funnier memory is that whenever there was some sickness "going around" my mother made me wear a little sack around my neck with garlic gloves in it. This remedy might have saved me from getting the usual childhood sicknesses, like measles, whooping cough, smallpox and whatever else children who go to school are exposed to, except that after these bouts of infectious illnesses had passed and all the other children were well again my mother let me go to school without the little garlic bag and I promptly got the illness which by then all the others had overcome.

Fortunately, I must have been born with fairly healthy genes and a positive outlook on life. Somehow I learned to cope with many of those difficulties and when I think about them today I believe the treatment I received strengthened me, and that subconsciously I probably enjoyed the attention I received, even if it was negative.

The schoolhouse, the *Volksschule* (people's school), was a two-storey building. On the lower floor lived one of the teachers, *Lehrer* (Teacher) Brenner and his wife. The upper floor had two rooms, one facing east and one facing west. In the room to the east were grades one to four. Their first teacher was Fräulein Schauss. When she left, she was replaced by Lehrer Schiff. In the western room were grades five to eight, with Lehrer Brenner. In each room there were about thirty-eight to forty students representing four different grades – an arrangement that was of great benefit to children in the lower grades: because they always were exposed to the subjects that were taught to the higher grades, they were never bored. When our turn came to move to the next grade we had already heard the topics and therefore nothing was really new to us, except in grades one and five.

Eight years was the obligatory standard education at this school level, but I was aiming for a higher education, a decision that had to be made after the completion of grade four. It was often a hard decision, because to go to high school one had to pay a monthly fee (*Schulgeld*). When I completed grade four in April 1929, my parents decided to send me to the *Oberrealschule* (high school) in Mainz, a city of 160,000 people, twenty-five kilometres from Dalheim. To get to the *Oberrealschule*, I had a daily one-and-a-half hour train ride. I had to get up at a quarter to 6:00 for breakfast, and then walk the fifteen minutes to the station, where I caught the 6:30 train. It was a local train, which took me to Nierstein am Rhein, where I had to change trains to the main line, which got me to Mainz by 5 minutes to 8:00. Because school started at 8:00, and because the school was a ten-minute walk from the railroad station, I always had to run to school. At 1:00 o'clock, I would take the train back, and, after missing connections, as I usually did, would be home by 3:30. This all was a little hard for a nine-year-old boy.

My mother was always a little worried about her little boy, though she never let me see it: outwardly, she showed great confidence in my ability to be a "big boy." One of her worries was that I was exposed daily to the occupation troops from France, Algiers and Morocco. They were mostly African Arabs, who traveled regularly on the same trains as I did and hung around the railroad stations. Those trains had single compartments holding about eight people each. My mother always warned me never to enter a compartment in which only soldiers were sitting. Of course, this could not always be avoided. The troops were there because as a condition of the Versailles Treaty the Rhineland to the western side of the Rhine River was occupied by French troops. It was the first time in my life that I saw people who looked different than I did. Most of the soldiers were dark-skinned, and some were very black, yet they did not scare me: I already knew black people existed, because I had a children's book, called *Der Struwwelpeter*, or "Shocking Peter." In it was the illustrated story of a black boy who got teased by three white boys. A "Big Nikolas," with a big inkwell, warned the white boys not to mock the black boy because of the colour of his skin, but they did not listen and continued to ridicule him. Finally, the "Big Nikolas" picked up the three white boys and dunked them in his inkwell: they came out even blacker than the black boy, which seemed to me to be proper justice! The Moroccan soldiers in their sloppily worn light beige uniforms were generally not liked very much. They were very different and were a daily reminder of the Occupation. Their difference intrigued me, though, and I accepted them. Looking back, it is remarkable that a pre-Hitler German children's author was so tolerant and tried to teach tolerance to German children. I don't think Hitler and his followers read *Der Struwwelpeter* when they were children.

When I was in the Italian Army as an interpreter and stationed in Kairouan in 1943, I met one of the Tunisians who had been stationed in Wiesbaden and Mainz during that time in 1929. I had never any problems with any of these soldiers. In fact, I thought most of them were kind. On them, I could practice the little bit of French I was starting to learn at the Oberrealschule, and they gave me French cigarettes, Gauloises, which I tried to smoke in the toilets at the railroad station. My mother did not know about that. The Gauloise cigarettes were coarse, sharp, bitter and extra cheap – made for the soldiers. They were certainly not inviting to smoke, but were used to show off and pretend to be grown up. With those things, there really was no chance of becoming addicted.

I felt quite proud to be going to high school, because it brought me admiration from my former classmates in the village, whose parents did not see the need to send them to high school, since, after all, most of them would stay on the farm. The transition from the country elementary school to the city high school, however, was quite a drastic one: up until then I was taught writing in the old, German gothic, calligraphic style, which is completely different from the Latin style which we all use today. What's more, terms for studying grammar, whether German or French, were suddenly in Latin, instead of the German language terminology I had learned for four years. For example, *Hauptwort* and *Tätigkeitswort* became the unfamiliar "noun" and "verb." It was very difficult, but I managed, though I had difficulty in French. When my parents received a notice during the Christmas break that I would have to improve my French or I would not pass in April, they debated for a long time whether they should continue to send me to the school. Ultimately, the main considerations were economic ones. When I started high school in April 1929, things were going pretty well in Germany and in the world as a whole, but in October 1929 the stock market crashed in the U.S.A. The entire world economy was affected, of course, but the post-war German economy completely collapsed. My parents could no longer afford the fees of twenty-one Marks for the school plus ten Marks for my monthly railroad pass. Thirty-one Marks was a lot of money, considering that a skilled labourer earned about six Marks in a nine-hour day. I returned to the Volksschule in Dalheim. It was a great blow to my ego, yet I had no choice but to accept my fate and make the best of it. I completed my eight years of elementary school with good grades, and in the back of my mind was the certainty that one day I would find time, ways and means to graduate from a high school and maybe even move on to university. My mother supported my dreams and used one of her ever-ready and fitting proverbs: "*Aufgeschoben ist nicht aufgehoben*" (postponed is not cancelled).

2. The Steel Helmets

The years following the 1929 stock market crash coincided with the rise of Adolf Hitler and his N.S.D.A.P. (*National Sozialistische Deutsche Arbeiter Partei* = National Socialist German Workers' Party). They also included my adolescence.

The small village of Dalheim was composed mainly of farmers, making what at that time was considered an average living. As was the case in most villages, the majority of the people of Dalheim became followers of Hitler. They believed Hitler's promises to get rid of unemployment and make Germany a respected world power again, wiping out the shame of the Versailles Treaty of 1919. With the entire village of the same political colour, there was no disharmony and no opposition. The few socialists in the village, who did reject Hitler, were mostly from poor families. Socially, they did not count. Life went on as usual, but there were subtle changes.

While I was still attending school in Mainz, a friend gave me a small lapel pin – a swastika. I wore it because I liked it as a decoration for my suit coat. I learned quickly the effect the symbol had on some people. My train trip to school involved a five-minute passage through a tunnel, during which the compartments were completely dark. One day I was in one of the eight-person compartments with other people, young and old. When we entered the tunnel, two or three people pounced on me, ripped off my swastika lapel pin and gave me a thorough beating, against which I was too small, weak and helpless to defend myself. When we emerged from the tunnel, everybody was sitting quietly as if nothing had happened. No one even looked at me. After that I did not wear swastika lapel pins.

During these times I felt jealous of my brother Bruno. When times had been better and money wasn't so tight, he had been able to further his education at the *Realschule* in Oppenheim, a city of about 5,000, which was only six kilometres from Dalheim. As an eleven-, twelve- and thirteen-year-old-boy in Dalheim, I went to school with friends who all belonged to the Hitler Youth Organization: the H.J., or the *Hitler Jugend*, and the *Jungvolk*, for the younger children. The Hitler Youth Organization had sport meets, marching drills, a band of drums and pipes, and an overall camaraderie that was appealing and appeared very wholesome. I wanted to participate in all of these activities and at the age of eleven or twelve made an application to join – without the knowledge of my parents, and against the wish of my father. He was never impressed with Hitler and his party.

As the Nazi movement grew stronger over the years before 1933, my father kept saying repeatedly, *"Armes, armes Deutschland, der Hitler will Krieg machen"* – (Poor, poor Germany, this Hitler wants to make war.) He sensed this, without having read Hitler's *Mein Kampf*, in which Hitler announced his intentions to the world. Nobody wanted to believe it; neither Hitler's followers in Dalheim, nor for that matter anybody who read that book at that time. To some extent, my father admired Mussolini for some of the good things he had done for Italy, as described in the Italian newspapers that my father occasionally read.

Influenced as I was by my friends in the school and the village, I did not agree with my father's sentiments and thought, "Well, the 'Old Man' doesn't know." But this skepticism on his part about Hitler planted a degree of caution in the back of my mind, and I was never really convinced that what was going on around me was for the best. From my friends I learned many of the catchy marching tunes and songs that extolled Germany and the Nazi movement, but I was never allowed to sing them in our house. I always remember the serious tone in which I was told that when I was outside the house with my friends I could sing them, but not in our house – ever. My application to join the Hitler Youth was rejected because I was not a German citizen. Since my father had preserved his Italian citizenship, although he had lived continuously in Germany since 1896, I was technically an Italian. At twelve years of age, I did not know how lucky I was.

In the September 1930 general election, Hitler's party won an unexpectedly large number of seats in the Reichstag. In a landslide, his Nazi Party went from twelve seats to one hundred and seven, and became the second largest party, after the SPD (Social Democratic Party). Hitler's Nazi Party formed a coalition with another very nationalistic party, the *Deutsch-Nationale Volks*

Partei (also called *Der Stahlhelm* - the Steel Helmets) under Huggenberg, and thereby altered the political landscape in the Reichstag. On January 30, 1933, the German Reich's President, Paul von Hindenburg, invited Hitler to form the government. That day marked the beginning of Germany's end, though only a very few people felt it at the time. I think my father was one of them. The people were told that it was the beginning of the "1000 Year Reich."

I was in grade eight at the time; in April I would graduate. Before Hitler became Chancellor of the Reich, we were not allowed to sing any Hitler songs, neither in class nor on the school grounds during recess, but after January 30th our teacher appeared in the classroom with a swastika *Parteiabzeichen* (party pin) on his lapel. From then on we were not only allowed to sing Hitler songs, but were actually encouraged to sing them. For convenience and to preserve his job, our teacher had had to join the party; he was actually a socialist.

That was the time when the German economy was at its lowest point. My father had very little work for his terrazzo and cement business. I was out of school at the age of thirteen and had to look for a job as an apprentice in some trade. Eventually I found a place in the office of a winery in Oppenheim, where I could train to become an office clerk. The winery was called *Heilig Geist Weinkellerei Wilhelm Nödling* – "Wilhelm Nödling's Holy Spirit Winery." I had to walk six kilometres to work every morning, which took about one hour, to be in the office by 8:00 a.m. There I started off doing some filing, and some sorting of papers, and started to learn to type, but as the days and the weeks went by I found myself more often working in the wine cellars: washing wine barrels and wine bottles, pouring wine and brandy into bottles, and labeling them. When alone in the cellar, I had many opportunities to sample the golden liquid that went into those bottles; as the days progressed I got a little tipsy and happier all the time. By the time I was ready to walk my six kilometres back home, at around 6:00 o'clock, I was a bit light-headed. That did not escape the attentive eye of my mother. Although she spoke to my boss about this, things did not change; after six weeks she did not let me go back to my job any more. I was not yet fourteen years old.

In June 1933, I started to work for my father, whenever he had a job to do. At the same time I looked in the newspaper for a job as an apprentice. For a time, I answered many ads without results. Finally, in February 1934, I was successful. That month, I wrote three letters in reply to three different ads for apprenticeship positions: one was for a cooper (barrel maker), one for a baker, and one for an office clerk. The last sentence in the first of my three applications read, "The greatest wish in my life has always been to become a cooper;" in the next, "to become a baker;" and in the other, "to become an office clerk." The baker, who was in Mainz, was the only one who answered. My brother Bruno accompanied me to the interview – after a twenty-four-kilometre bicycle trip to Mainz. There, the *Bäckermeister* (master baker) Herr August Nickel told us that I was one of one hundred and fifty applicants and that he would notify me in due time after he had interviewed some of the others. A week later I was informed that he had decided on me and that I should come with one of my parents to make a *Lehrvertrag* (apprenticeship contract) for a period of three years, from March 1934 to March 1937. My father and my mother came with me and we all signed. The conditions were as follows: I would get room and board for six days a week, and one Mark per week in wages during the first year, two Marks per week the second year, and three Marks per week during the third year. On Saturday night at 7:30 I had to take the train to go home for Sunday. On Sunday night I had to be back to work by 7:00 p.m., to prepare for Monday morning: cleaning baking pans, preparing dough-making equipment, and calculating and weighing out the ingredients for the next day's dough. The one Mark per week I earned in the first year was just enough for traveling home and back again to work: the return ticket cost ninety-five Pfennigs. That left me five Pfennigs to buy myself a stick of peppermint candy, which I did. It was not all that bad, though, because my father gave me one Mark each week to replace the one I had used for my railroad tickets.

The working and living conditions during the three years of my apprenticeship were much different from what I was accustomed to. There was a youth workers' protection law in place at the time, which stated that an apprentice was not allowed to work longer than forty-eight hours in a week and, for as long he was still under sixteen years of age, must not start working before 6:00 a.m. These conditions were not met in this bakery. I started working every weekday morning at 4:00 a.m. By 7:00 a.m., I was on the bicycle with a basket full of buns to be delivered to various customers all over the city of Mainz – through the busy city traffic of cars and streetcars, and dodging the dangerous rail grooves in the pavement. This route was repeated in the afternoon with bread. Breakfast was eaten in the bakery, after the morning rounds, usually by 8:00 a.m. The midday meal was eaten in a small room above the bakery. We sat down only as long as it took to eat. The food was adequate in quantity and average in quality, but not like at home. Work usually ended between 2:00 and 4:00 p.m., depending on the amount of bread and buns that were needed for the day. On some days during the middle of the week, when we were not too busy and finished a little early, the master's wife had us wash the tile walls of the bakery or found some other chores for us to do to fill those empty hours in the afternoon.

The sleeping quarters were inadequate. A journeyman and three apprentices slept in one room, in which four beds were cramped together with barely enough room to pass between them. A wardrobe was also in the room, which took away even more space. The room had an angled ceiling with a small gable window. The total floor space was not more than three meters by five meters, at the most. What's more, in my first year-and-a-half at the bakery I was never allowed to go out. It was almost like being in a prison, but it did keep me out of trouble. The rare times that I finished a little earlier, and if I had some money left over from what my father had given me, I could ask permission to see a movie, maybe from 5:00 to 7:00 p.m., but even on those evenings I had to be back by 7:00 to do the hour's preparatory work for the next day.

In the third year it was a little easier to get permission to go out for a couple of hours and wander through the city, which I did on many occasions. At that time my brother Bruno was working as a sailor on a Dutch Rhine barge. He had bought himself a riding outfit made of a black-and-white chequered fabric. The suit included breeches, coat, cap and black riding boots. Since he decided not to wear it, he gave it to me. I, who certainly did not have many clothes, was thrilled with the gift. Since I always wanted to project the best possible image of myself, I wore this outfit on my walks through the city, pretending to be somebody I was not. To add a little spice to the image, I bought myself a false black moustache and glued it under my nose. I still have it and even used it once more at a masked ball in Canada.

That third year was also when I started to smoke. I was drawn to it because of the movies. I saw how the hero, who had won the heart of the leading lady, would pull out his gold or silver cigarette case, offer a cigarette to his lady, and then pull one out for himself. Then he would snap the case closed and tap the cigarette on the lid of the case, flick his lighter, elegantly light the lady's cigarette and then his own. These gestures were incredibly sophisticated, including the flipping off of the ashes. With these gestures, the hero would completely dominate the scene; I felt if I behaved likewise, I, too, would have a good start in the "high life" with the ladies, or, at the worst, would at least not harm anyone.

In that third year, when I turned seventeen, I had my first "grown up" sense of what love might be. Across the narrow back alley from our second storey window were the windows of another apartment. From time to time I saw a pretty young girl looking out of one of these windows. Whenever I saw her I waved at her, but like a properly brought-up girl she ignored me and did not respond. It was too far and too impractical to shout across the alley, so I just kept waving at her, until one day she waved back. From then on we made signs to each other, trying to communicate, and one day, on a Saturday, I let her know that I was free a little earlier than usual and would like to walk with her in the park near the railroad station.

We met at the station two hours before my train was due to leave and very shyly introduced ourselves. Her name was Kätchen (Kitty) Federizzi and she was my age or a little younger. We walked and talked about a lot of innocent things, until we came to the topic of love. We really liked each other and at this point said so. Then we sat down on a park bench, first apart, then a little closer, and before we knew what was happening we kissed. What a revelation to me – to her maybe, too. After a little while, I asked her if I might hold her lovely little breast and she said shyly: "Yes, once." I was drunk with bliss. By this point, though, it was time to catch my train: we kissed once more and said good-bye. It was a touching, innocent experience that I have never forgotten. We never walked together again, as she was strictly controlled by her parents and I could not always get away early enough. Not long after that lovely encounter, I finished my apprenticeship, passed my exams, and left Mainz to take on a position as a pastry maker volunteer in a bakery and pastry shop in Darmstadt, to further my experience (I received ten Marks per week as a baker, but my two hours every day in the pastry shop were unpaid!), so that I would have a better chance to get a good job in the future.

My exams were a practical and theoretical exam prescribed by state law. During the three years of apprenticeship, I had attended a trade school two afternoons per week (Mondays and Tuesdays from 2:00 to 4:00 p.m.), where apprentices learned not only about baking chemistry but also about how to run a business, the prevailing business laws, and accounting. Of the fifty or so apprentices who were taking the exams, I was one of the three best. For this, I won an award: besides a handsome diploma, I received a book, *Hitler Junge Quex*, a story about a nice German boy's life as a member of the Hitler Youth organization. I don't know exactly what happened to this book; most likely my parents disposed of it.

An event I also remember was the entrance of German troops, in March 1936, into the Demilitarized Zone of the Rhineland – which included Mainz. It was one of Hitler's goals to occupy this demilitarized part of Germany. My father said: "This is the time when France and Britain should give Hitler an ultimatum and stop him and his military ambitions." But they did not, and thereby encouraged Hitler to carry on his dangerous game of defying the world. He bluffed regarding the number of troops that entered Mainz. One soldier I spoke to marched three times into Mainz by day to stage the occupation of the Demilitarized Zone, and rode two times back out by night.

During the third year of my apprenticeship, I bought a two-seater *Paddelboot* (canoe) to use on the Rhine. I bought it for thirty Marks from another baker journeyman, who had just finished his apprenticeship. It took me ten weeks to pay for it by using my total pay for that period. I had it moored at a yacht club in a harbour on the Rhine, which also cost some money, so I was in debt for some time. I used it a few times on Sundays. When I had a one-week holiday, I paddled about twenty kilometres up the Rhine, towards Nierstein – close to my home. I got a serious sunburn early on and cured it during the week holiday, then paddled back, down the Rhine the following Sunday. I sold the boat again when I moved to Darmstadt.

By the time I had finished my apprenticeship in March 1937, the German economy had started to boom, and to find a job in a bakery with a pastry shop was easy. Because I had lived three years in Mainz, I wanted a change of scenery. I had always wanted to live in and experience big cities, so as my next city of work and residence I chose Darmstadt. It felt familiar and comfortable, because my father had opened his first independent business there, between 1900 and 1905 or thereabouts.

3. Chocolate-Covered Pralines

On June 9, 1937, I started working for the *Bäckerei & Konditorei Fritz Ihrig* (Fritz Ihrig's Bakery and Pastry Shop) in Darmstadt. I was now a journeyman and pastry volunteer, and had room and board, plus ten Marks a week. The treatment was much kinder and more respectful than at my apprenticeship, the accommodation was much better, and I had freedom: I could go out when work was finished. The hours were a regular forty-eight-hours per week. I could even buy some better clothes. My brother gave me English fabric as a present, from which I had a tailored suit made.

As a baker, my days started at 4:00 in the morning (at 2:00 on Saturdays), while the afternoons were free. With the free time and money to afford nice clothes and other luxuries, I began to experience the finer side of city life. On occasion, I enjoyed myself in reputable *Tanz Cafés* (dance cafes), where orchestras were playing. I also saw my first operas and went to plays in the theatre.

During my time in Darmstadt, I attended a *Tanz-Schule* (a dance school), where I learned to dance. I also learned the social graces that were expected of an educated "world-wise" young man. At the end of the session, the dance school put on a final ball. I had to have calling cards printed, so that I could properly invite a girl, also a student of the class. To make the invitation, I had to make an appointment with her and her parents for a Sunday morning around 11:00 o'clock. When I called on them, a young woman – not a family member – opened the door. I gave her my calling card to announce my arrival. She invited me in and led me to a reception area. After I had waited for a few minutes, the mother and my dance partner came to greet me. I stated the reason for my call, and with her mother's consent the young lady graciously accepted my invitation. After a short visit, I excused myself and departed, content to have found approval from the girl's mother and, of course, from the girl herself.

For the ball, each gentleman had to bring some sort of gift, possibly something that would be humorous. Since I worked as a pastry chef, and could make chocolate-covered pralines, I found a proper box and put some good pralines in it. Then I also made some special ones by gathering some clean wood shavings, making round balls out of them and coating them with good chocolate. These I placed between the good ones in the box. There were many surprises, and those who got the good ones laughed when they saw the others struggling with the chocolate-coated wood shavings and trying to get rid of them in an inconspicuous way. Today I think it was rather mean, but back then there was much laughter, and no great harm was done. No one held it against me.

While in Darmstadt, I saw terrazzo floors my father had laid at the turn of the century. I recognized them because in his mosaic decorations he had incorporated his initials, D.R. (Domenico Redivo). He had had a thriving business there and had produced highly valued work, but because he was not proficient enough in the German language at the time he had to rely on a German accountant for his bookkeeping. This accountant cheated him out of money by manipulating the books. By the time my father discovered the embezzlements it was too late to save the business. He left Darmstadt around 1904 and returned to Wiesbaden, where his bride was waiting for him. They got married in 1905. My father started a new business and continued to work in his trade. This time, though, he did not want to depend on an accountant, so his wife did his office work and accounting – an easy job for her because of her experience as a stenography clerk at the *Wiesbadener Kourier*, the most important daily newspaper of Wiesbaden, a city of about 100,000 at that time.

Having tasted the experience of living in a big city, and having turned eighteen during my time in Darmstadt, I became more aware of not being German: all my school chums were doing their military service, whereas I wasn't, because I was an Italian citizen. It was at that time that I started to wear a lapel pin with the Italian flag and a *fascio* (the insignia of Mussolini's party) on it. When people noticed and asked me about it, I pretended to be an Italian student. By chance I met the son of another *Italiano all'Estero* (an Italian expatriate), who told me about the Italian community in Frankfurt. As an Italian citizen I could get lessons in Italian there, but I would first have to join the Young Fascist group. As a member of this group, though, I could go to summer camps in Rome, free of charge, and be supplied with an elegant uniform. I was very interested in taking advantage of these free offers, without which I could never dream of going to Italy. I did not think of the political implications.

In April 1938, I left my place of work in Darmstadt and went to Wiesbaden. I took a position there with the *Bäckerei Johann Damm*. Again I improved my situation: there were better working conditions, better accommodations and better pay. While in Wiesbaden I continued to have spare time in the afternoons and evenings and took up playing chess every day at the *Café Lodroner*. The owner, Mr. Lodroner, had once been a finalist in the German Chess Championship, and was still very good. During my time there I even had the chance to watch the reigning German chess champion play simultaneously against forty top local players. He won all his games except two, both of which ended in a draw.

While I was living in Wiesbaden I also began to attend Italian classes, conducted by an officer of the Fascist Party. No political indoctrination took place during these lessons; they were strictly Italian language lectures. It was during one class that our instructor, Lt. Innocenti, asked who would be available to go to a Young Fascist summer camp in Rome for two weeks. I was anxious to go. I asked my employer if I could get a leave of absence, an extension of my stipulated holidays. When he said yes, I was very excited. Once I registered to become a member of the group that would go to Rome, I was automatically inscribed into the *Giovani Fascisti* (Young Fascist) organization. I received a wonderful uniform: black shirt, black tunic, black breeches, black riding boots, black uniform hat with frilly tassels and the fascio in gold, and a black cape. It all looked very impressive on me. Dressed like that, I left my country for the first time in my life, to travel to Italy, my father's country of origin, and to Rome, the Holy City. I had just turned nineteen.

I liked Italy and its people instantly and I felt Italian the moment I crossed over the Austrian border at the Brenner Pass. It was early, about 5:00 o'clock in the morning, when I looked out of the train and for the first time in my life saw really big mountains. The trip to Rome, almost the length of the entire "boot" through that strange and constantly varying countryside, was an experience I have never forgotten. I did not know at that time that I would travel that stretch many more times during my life, by car as well as by train.

During our time at camp we played games, were taken a few times to the Mediterranean beach in Ostia, and ate well. We were first accommodated in tents, then in a school at the foot of the Via Nomentana, in a neighbourhood called Monte Mario. From what I remember, we received neither military training nor any fascist indoctrination. It was strictly a summer camp for *Figli di Italiani all'Estero* (Sons of Italians in Foreign Countries). We came from all the European countries and the rim of the Mediterranean: Egypt, Tunisia, Libya, Algiers, and the Middle East. This exposure to a different country, Italy, and to people from so many other countries broadened my outlook considerably, even though communication was limited because of the language barrier. When I arrived, I had taken only about six or seven lessons, and was an absolute beginner. My knowledge of Italian was as good as non-existent.

Only one event in the four weeks I was there could be termed political. It was a review, by Mussolini himself, of probably five to six hundred of us youth in Piazza Siena in Rome. We had to shine our boots and get our uniforms in immaculate condition. Around 8:00 in the morning we were driven to the piazza and placed in our positions in preparation for when il Duce would come to review us and speak to us. We waited all morning and rehearsed again and again our routines and the shouting of *"Viva il Duce!"* and *"Duce, Duce, Duce!"* We also sang patriotic songs, which we had learned during our time at the camp. Finally, around 2:00 p.m., il Duce arrived and spoke to us for about fifteen minutes. It was a speech many of us did not understand. Then we returned to camp. As far as I remember, il Duce's words did not leave an impression on me. I did not understand what he had said and I was pretty tired and fed up with all the waiting we had to do for a fifteen-minute speech.

As it turned out, for those of us who came from Frankfurt, which was quarantined with a polio epidemic, the two weeks became four. The extra time allowed me to fall even more in love with Italy, its people and its food. I liked everything. From street stands in Rome I bought fresh watermelons, oranges and other fruits, the best I ever ate. That was also where I ate my first raw mussels with fresh lemon. They were under stands in a bucket of water, alive; the vendor would pick them out, open them with a knife, and put lemon on them. I would let them slide down my throat with gusto.

4. *Princess Mafalda*

After my return from Rome I continued making bread and pastries at the bakery in Wiesbaden. One morning in the fall, on September 9, 1938, in fact, while out on my morning route delivering buns I heard noises in the main shopping area of the city and saw smoke rising over the houses in a nearby street. My curiosity got the better of me and I pedaled my bicycle over to investigate. I was appalled and frightened to see that the big show windows of big fine stores were being smashed and looted. Pieces of furniture were thrown down on the sidewalks from the windows of some houses. The people involved were shouting obscenities and cursing the Jews. Other people were just quietly standing at a distance. They watched this ravaging unfold without doing anything about it. To me this was an event I could not understand. As I discovered later, the smoke came from the synagogue, which was on fire nearby. This was the infamous *Kristalnacht*, the Night of Broken Glass, organized and perpetrated by the Nazi private army, the S.A. (*Sturm Abteilung*, or "the Brown Shirts") on the pretence that it was a spontaneous uprising in response to the killing in Paris of the Third Secretary of the German Embassy, Ernst von Rath, by the seventeen-year old Polish Jew Hershl Grynszpan. This was the first time that I became consciously aware of the persecution of the Jews in Germany. From that time on I began to understand my father's dislike for Hitler and his party. After Kristalnacht, no more Italian language classes were offered.

I worked in that bakery in Wiesbaden until the end of March 1939. At that time the German economy was better than it had been for many years and my father had plenty of work in his business. Because I had worked for him briefly when I had finished school at thirteen, he asked me to work for him again and eventually take over the business. My older brother Bruno had also worked for our father from time to time, but the two did not get along, so there was no possibility that Bruno would take over. In fact, Bruno had started his own business, in competition with our father. This was in 1938, when the summit meeting of Hitler, Mussolini, Daladier and Chamberlain was held in Munich. The topic of discussion was the annexation of the Sudetenland, the largely German-speaking western regions of Czechoslovakia; in order to avoid a war, Daladier and Chamberlain agreed with Hitler, and part of Czechoslovakia was annexed to Germany. Austria had already been annexed peacefully earlier in the same year. Once again, the Munich meeting made me believe that Hitler wanted peace, but my father said that Hitler was going to start a war. To settle it, I bet a bottle of wine with my father that there would be no war. Little did I know that on September 1, 1939 I would lose that bet. That's when the Blitzkrieg against Poland began, under what we now know were false pretences, with a fabricated border incident at Gleiwitz, on the German-Polish border.

Only a few days later, news of the village's first casualty reached Dalheim. A dear school friend of mine was reported killed in action. Because I was of Italian nationality, I had not been drafted into the German Army. All those I went to school with, though, had just finished their two years of compulsory military service, were still in the Army, and were the first ones to be thrown into combat. These events affected me profoundly, but there was nothing I could do about them.

My partnership with my father did not work out. My father was a master in his trade, but not a good businessman, and although my mother could keep the books and look after all the office work, she could work only with the information she received from her husband regarding expenses, income and whatever had to do with record keeping. As a result, there were times when things went well and others when they didn't. I did not like this instability, but instead of arguing with my father, as my brother had done, I decided just to leave on friendly terms and find a job as baker again in a big city. Besides, I liked the atmosphere of big city life.

On December 29, 1939 I arrived in Frankfurt with very little money. My father had not paid me well for my work and, what's more, I had spent all of my weekly earnings before each week was out. It was only natural: I was young and wanted to enjoy myself. The funny part of it was that my father had been in the habit of borrowing some of Bruno's wages on Monday mornings to buy materials for new jobs. He had paid Bruno and me on Saturday or Sunday mornings, and because we were his children he thought he could ask us to lend him the money back on Monday or Tuesday. My brother used to give it to him, sometimes never getting it back, whereas I didn't. I could honestly say that I didn't have any money left, because I had spent it all on the Sunday!

When I reached Frankfurt, I had no difficulty in finding a job right away. I started working on January 4, 1940 for *Ludwig Eckert Bäckerei* in Frankfurt-Sachsenhausen. Because most young and qualified workers were in the Army and at the Front, I was a great asset: I would not be called up. Adolf Brambilla, another *figlio di Italiani all'Estero*, worked at the same place. Because of our unique status, and because we worked at the same establishment, we became friends. After work we used to eat together in a restaurant in the neighbourhood. After Italy declared war on France in May 1941, an elderly waiter there told us that if Mussolini had decided to enter the war on the Allied side he would have had us strung up on the nearest lamppost. And he said it in all seriousness. So, in one sense we were lucky; in another it would have been better for us if Italy had not entered the war at all and had stayed neutral like Spain.

Throughout my life I have had a constant and unbelievable amount of luck, starting with my parents' move to the country when I was a baby. After that, as an Italian citizen I was not allowed to join the Hitler Youth, nor could I be drafted into the German Army. This good luck came about because of the German law that children born in Germany do not become German citizens but take on the nationality of their father. My other bit of luck is that in 1923 my father had applied to become a naturalized German citizen. He did it because he was bidding on a big government contract, which could be awarded only to a German firm. His application for citizenship had to be approved unanimously by the village council. One of the councillors refused to endorse the application. Although it was suggested to my father that he change residence, at least on paper, to the nearby little city of Oppenheim, where all the city councillors knew him well and assured him that his application would pass, he was too proud and said, "If they don't want me, I don't need them." He remained Italian – and so did his children. As a result, my brother, Bruno, although also of military age, did not have to join the German Army either and gainfully worked in his own business throughout the war years.

Working in Ludwig Eckert's Bakery turned out not to be much fun, because there was a rather elderly co-worker who teased me constantly and gave me a hard time during the whole work shift, all because I was Italian, was neither in the Army nor in the war, and did not openly demonstrate support for Hitler. He could not leave me alone. I first ignored the situation, but when it became worse I contemplated looking for work in another bakery. Working against me was a wartime law stipulating that no employee could change jobs without the consent of his employer. In other words, you could not quit your job if your boss did not want to let you go. I was a good worker, so I had to stay. Fortunately, I was in Frankfurt, where the Italian Consulate General was located. Once again, I had a chance to take up my Italian Lessons – sponsored, as before, by the Young Fascist organization. It was my first contact with this Italian youth group since my month in Rome. The possibility hadn't existed during the year I spent working for my father in Dalheim; the village was too small and too isolated. The language classes were held in the Casa d'Italia, which housed the consulate, and while attending them I got to know some German-speaking employees of the consulate. To one gentleman, Signor Cannobi, I explained my dilemma of not being able to seek employment in another bakery. When he heard this, he asked if I would consider taking on a job at the Italian Consulate. Of course I was delighted with this prospect, but could not see how this would be possible without a thorough knowledge of Italian. Signor Cannobi said that this would not be a problem, because they needed someone who was fluent in German and could deal with any outside errands and with Germans who came to the consulate: I could deal with them as a receptionist, then direct them to the right department in the consulate, and could learn Italian as well. I accepted the job immediately. As a member of the Italian Diplomatic Service, Signor Cannobi intervened on my behalf with the *Arbeitsamt* (the Workers Office) for my immediate release from the bakery, to be able to start my job with the Italian Consulate General on November 1, 1941.

Before proceeding to tell of my life at the consulate, I must relate an incident I experienced with my friend, Adi Brambilla. Since we worked in the same bakery, we spent some of our spare time together, mostly playing chess. Being a native of Frankfurt, he knew many people, including Jewish families, and one day invited me to come with him to the ghetto to visit two of the families who were forced to live there. It was the first time that I became fully aware of how great the plight of these people was. The husbands and fathers of these two families were professional musicians; until Hitler came to power they had played with the Frankfurt Opera Orchestra. After that, they were denied work with any orchestra or music group, so they fled to Holland to earn a living and to provide for the families they had to leave alone in Frankfurt and to whom they regularly sent money and food parcels. When I visited these families with Brambilla it was May 1940, just before the invasion of Holland. Each of these families had a teenage daughter. Brambilla suggested we visit them and offer to take the girls to a movie in the evening when it was dark and we would not draw any attention. To make it possible, they had to remove the yellow Star of David, which the law said they had to wear all the time when in public. Of course, officially they were not allowed to remove their stars, but they took the chance in order to go out with us.

We did go to the movies, but I shall never forget the anxiety we all experienced during those two hours and the subsequent dark walk home to their apartments at eleven o'clock through the rather deserted streets of the ghetto. After we said good night to the girls and were a few steps away from the entrance of the house where we left them, two men approached us and in a very rough way asked for our identification papers. Of course, as Italian citizens we always carried our passports with us. After examining our passports with flashlights the men murmured some insulting words and gave them back. We assumed that if we had carried German ID's we would have been arrested on the spot. We visited the families a few more times, but only in daylight when the streets were not so deserted. Since the families were always in need, they offered to sell us their husbands' clothes. I bought an overcoat at a fair price from the mother of Edith, the girl I had befriended at that time. I lost contact with her, and when I came back to Frankfurt for the first time after the war, in November 1945, and inquired about the families, there was no trace of them. It was obvious that they too had been transported to the East and had disappeared in the Holocaust.

With my new job at the consulate, my status in Germany changed. Until then, I had to obtain a *Befreiungsschein* every year, a permission paper for foreigners to work in Germany. Now, I did not need one any more; I was attached to the diplomatic service of Italy and therefore extraterritorial: I had no more taxes to pay and my income had soared from thirty-six Marks a week (without room and board) to a little more than three hundred Marks a month, without any deductions. I changed residence from where I lived in Sachsenhausen near the bakery and rented a room in Frankfurt proper, in the vicinity of the consulate. One of the major improvements of my new situation was that my food ration coupons changed from the usual war ration quantities to the diplomatic quantities, which were generously based on normal peacetime consumption of butter, meat, sugar, coffee, liqueurs, tobacco, and so on. On those rations, members of the consulate were living an enviable life in this Germany at war. Of course, with these extra ration coupons I could be generous. I shared them with my family and friends. Understandably, I became very popular with all of them. Not all was roses, though, because being a healthy and fit-looking young man I often received disapproving looks on the street, in streetcars, restaurants or at the movies, and sometimes was even asked why I was not a soldier in uniform like all the other German youth. At that time only criminals and unfit people with diseases or otherwise undesirable were not called up to serve in the army.

My work at the consulate was satisfying, even though I did not speak Italian. The Consul General at the time was Marchese Serra di Cassano, and his wife was the Contessa Brandolin of the Veneto region. They both were close friends of the royal family of Italy, King Vittorio Emanuele di Savoia and Queen Elena, a princess of Montenegro. One of their daughters, Princess Mafalda, who was married to Prince Philip of Hesse, was visiting Germany and holidaying in Bad Orb, and was to be picked up from there by car. The Consul sent his car, a Lancia, with his Italian driver to pick her up, but because the driver did not speak German I was sent with him in case there was a need for him to communicate with Germans at checkpoints or for car repairs, or whatever else came up. Thus I had the honour to meet this Italian Princess. She spoke German well and we carried on a normal conversation. She inquired about my family and me and encouraged me to learn Italian. After the war, I learned that she had been put into a German concentration camp because her husband was under the suspicion of having been part of the conspiracy to assassinate Hitler on July 20, 1944. She died in Buchen-Belsen under an air attack by the British.

My Italian made only slow progress. To force myself to improve more quickly, I agreed to take part in a play, *Le tre Grazie* (The Three Graces), which was put on by the youth group of the Italian colony. I had a lead role and I learned all my lines without really knowing the meaning of what I was saying. My teacher, and the director of the play, encouraged and helped me. My part was to be the father of triplets. I was directed to act a little ignorant, which I really was! Because I did not know what I was saying and therefore my appearance was quiet genuine, I had great success and received much applause.

In May 1942, after six months on my new job at the consulate, there came an order from the Ministry of War in Rome that all *Figli d'Italiani all'Estero* with birth years from 1917 to 1923 must report to their residence in Italy (their father's place of origin) to render six months of military service. It was implied that after the six months they could all go home again. This regulation applied to all those of Italian nationality living in Germany, Austria and all the countries occupied by the Germans, and of course the neutral countries like Switzerland and Sweden. Those who refused would be declared deserters and could never go to Italy without facing charges. What's more, they would not get their passports renewed and could then be expelled from their host country. The personnel manager, Dr. Papini, explained this to me, but added that if I did not want to go he could get an exemption, because I was part of the diplomatic service of the Foreign Ministry. However, he suggested it would be a good idea if I did go, because after six months in Italy I would become fluent in Italian. He also told me that if the army did not release me after the six months, as it had implied, the consulate could request my immediate release. The decision was left up to me. It was the time when the German and Italian war conquests were at their highest point: almost all of Europe was under German and Italian control. Up to then, there were hardly any air raids over the city of Frankfurt, and Germany seemed to be a pretty safe place, considering that the world was at war. The same applied to Italy, and since I was always a little curious and adventurous I felt it would be both safe and sensible to go to Italy for six months. Dr. Papini and my colleagues congratulated me on my decision and wished me good luck. I was happy and with great anticipation looked forward to my new adventure and the experiences that awaited me. So, on June 12, 1942, I left Germany for Italy, after saying good-bye to my parents and friends.

I also said good-bye to a girl friend, Margot Reinhard, with whom I had a romantic but platonic relationship while I was still living in Sachsenhausen and working in the bakery. My room there in Sachsenhausen was on the fourth floor, at number 43 Stegstrasse. Margot lived with her father and a stepmother in the street-level apartment of number 41. At first we saw each other often but did not greet or talk, until one day I found a note, a poem, in my mailbox, signed only with the initials "M. R." I concluded it could only be from this pretty blond girl I had been looking at all this time, and thought of how I could approach her in a proper way. With my luck, she solved the problem. However, I also discovered that although I was twenty-one, she was only sixteen years old. We had to meet on the sly, because her father would not tolerate any young man near his daughter, which was understandable. It was rather difficult for us to meet and enjoy each other's company. One time, the father surprised us while we were walking arm in arm in a neighbourhood park. That time, he chased me away – literally. Shortly afterwards, I got my job at the Italian Consulate and moved away from Stegstrasse to Westendstrasse in Frankfurt proper. From then on Margot and I saw less of each other, but we did stay in touch. She had finished school and had taken on a job as an accounting apprentice in the office of an important import and export carpet company. When we said our good-byes before I left for Italy, we confirmed our love for each other, but agreed that because of the uncertainties of the war we would not promise to wait for each other, so that we would not have to feel guilty if we met someone else during our separation. We promised, however, to write to each other regularly. Unfortunately, our letters never reached their destinations: while in the military in Italy I was always at different addresses; for her part, her father intercepted my mail and she never saw it.

My father accompanied me to the train station in Frankfurt. As a last parental gesture he handed me a *Zwanzigmarkschein* (twenty Mark bill) for the trip. Little did I know or suspect that I would not see him or Germany any more for the next four years and five months.

5. An Italian Soldier

On the 12th of June 1942, I reported to the Military District of Udine for my medical examination and was found fit for military service. After the examination, the military doctor asked me to what branch of the forces I wanted to be assigned: Army, Navy or Air Force? Since I had no preference and trusted fate, I asked him to decide. He thought for a minute and then asked me if I had relatives anywhere in Italy. When I said yes, at Roveredo in Piano, near Pordenone, he said, "Well then: *l. Reggimento Artiglieria Celere Pordenone.* This way, when you have a weekend pass and are free you can visit your relatives in Roveredo in Piano. That is only seven kilometres away from your barracks." Had this been the German Army, the medical officer most likely would not have had that compassion, and probably would have assigned me to a location far from relatives, to avoid the new soldier being pampered by family.

The artillery regiment to which I was assigned was at one time horse-drawn. By the time I arrived it was motorized and active on the front in Russia. In the barracks were the new recruits like myself, being trained as replacements for the losses incurred in the East. Since I was unaware of the conditions at the front, it did not bother me to know that I had to go to there. I was assigned and trained as a *Gognometrista*, a specialist who calculates the trajectory of the projectiles to be shot out of the cannons. My Italian was not very good at all, but I managed. On our first Sunday morning, all the recruits attended Catholic mass, from which I was excused because I was not Catholic but Protestant. Instead of being free during that time, however, I was assigned to clean the latrines. On subsequent Sundays I attended mass like everyone else!

On Sunday afternoons we were given passes and I could visit my relatives, whom I met for the first time in my life and of whom I really knew nothing, because my father neither talked about them nor had much contact with them. As he told us, this was because when their father died one of his half-brothers, Luigi, who had a career as *Maresciallo dei Carabinieri* (Police Staff Sergeant) and was *Podestà* (Mayor) of Roveredo in Piano, cheated him out of some of his rightful part of the inheritance. By the time I met those relatives, however, Luigi had already died; I was visiting with his widow, Italia, their two sons, Achille, eighteen, and Silvano, fifteen, and an aunt, Zia Maria, also a half-sister of my father. They were all very kind to me and I felt at home.

Two or three weeks after my arrival at the barracks, there came a request for typists. Since during the time I had been working in the bakery I had taken a touch-typing course in the afternoons at a Frankfurt Commerce School, I applied for a typing position. Days went by, and it was soon time for us to go on manoeuvres to be readied for our departure to Russia. The first part of our training was a forced march of about twenty-five to thirty kilometres, with all our personal equipment and our rifles. The rifles were rather small and not too heavy, because the artillery had cannons – for artillerists, the rifles were rather secondary. Actually, we had never fired them. When we arrived at our destination at Tarzo, we put the cannons into firing position. It was shortly after noon when an orderly came to look for Redivo Ugo to report immediately to the barracks of an infantry regiment in Vittorio Veneto. The orderly drove me there, and when I arrived I was told to wait for some others. Once they arrived in a few days time, we would have to submit to a typist examination. Meanwhile, those of us who were waiting had no duties to perform. We played cards and learned songs – some military ones, but mostly others extolling the beauty of love and life. One night we went out on passes and hiked high up to a village in the mountains, where we had heard there would be a dance. Our passes were good until 11:00 p.m., but we stayed a little longer and only got back after midnight. The sergeant in charge of the guard at the barrack gates arrested us. After taking away our belts, shoelaces and le Stellette, the stars that every soldier wears on his uniform to symbolize military discipline, he put us in jail. The next morning we were thoroughly reprimanded, but once we mentioned where we had been and what we done – dancing with girls – there were no other consequences. That was the Italian Army!

After about three weeks of idly waiting, the day of the exam finally arrived. An officer started dictating war bulletins and other military texts. I touch-typed quickly, and the officer was impressed by my speed. After he had finished dictating, he started to take one sheet after another out of the type-writers and examined them. When he came to my sheet he looked at it with anticipation, but then I saw him shake his head again and again. Finally he came back to me and said, "*Peccato*, what a pity. You can type, but you don't know Italian. Therefore you have to go back to Pordenone and your regiment." Later, I learned that those who passed the exam were sent to Montenegro, an area occupied by the Italians and infested with partisans, who inflicted daily casualties on the Italians stationed there.

When I returned to my regiment in Pordenone, all the others with whom I had trained had left for Russia. I was re-assigned to the next replacement group, with more new recruits. The degree of committment these recruits and many other Italians had to this war can be seen by the questions they asked me: "Ugo," they would ask me, "you come from Germany and seem to be in-telligent. Can you tell us against whom we are in the war and why?" When I said it was against Great Britain and Russia, they would ask, "But what have they done to us that we must fight them?" Frankly, I never found a good an-swer to such a simple question. But in a way I still thought the Axis should and would win the war. This would all change after one of my visits to my relatives in Roveredo.

On the Sunday when I arrived, my aunt Maria was away. When I remarked on this I was told, "Oh, she is out in the fields collecting something for lunch." I did not pay further attention, but asked what we would have for lunch. The answer was *"polenta col toccio,"* meaning the usual polenta and some kind of sauce with it. Eventually, after my aunt Maria had returned from the fields, lunch was served and eaten. The *toccio* was very good, a spicy tomato sauce with some delicious meat chunks. After we finished, I was asked if I liked what I ate. When I answered in the affirmative, they asked if I knew what it was. I said no, but would like to know. So they explained that Zia Maria had been out all morning collecting snails in the fields, and that is what we had eaten. Having never eaten snails before and having been introduced to this delicacy in this manner, I was quite pleased with myself.

When visiting my aunts another time – with whom, by now, I could com-municate very well – I had an experience that changed my whole outlook on life. The news from the radio, of which I could understand quite a bit but not all, gave a report from the Russian Front, where the Germans had encircled and "annihilated" so many thousand Russians. On hearing this "victory news," I shouted "Hooray! Another victory for us!" Both my aunts looked at me angrily and said: "Ugo, shame on you! How can you shout 'Hooray' when so many people have died?" Sheepishly, I said, "but they are enemies," upon which they answered, "What do you mean enemies? They are people like you: sons of their mothers, husbands of their wives, brothers of their sisters, fathers of children who will never see them again! How can you be jubilant at such news?" These simple and compassionate women woke me up and made me think.

Before this incident, I was disciplined in behaviour and dressed as a German soldier would: always cleanly and properly, with polished shoes and pressed pants. The lieutenant who commanded our company often cited me in front of everyone as a disciplined soldier and an example of proper appearance. After the enlightening incident with my aunts, however, I stopped cleaning my boots and pressing my pants, and began to look like my comrades from all over Italy. After a week or so of this, the commanding officer of the company approached me from behind one day, put his arm around my shoulder, and said, "Now, Redivo, you are an Italian soldier. Now I like you." From that day on, he took me out many times to the café downtown to play chess with him. This was a beautiful time and I learned to enjoy everything Italian. I had saved some money in Germany, which I had sent to me in care of my aunt Italia. It was about 425 Reichsmarks, which gave me 3000 Lire, a nice sum in those times, considering that a good meal and a bottle of wine was about 15 to 20 Lire. I kept spending as long as I had the money, not thinking of the future, or that my parents could not send me any more money because of the restrictions on foreign exchange in Germany.

I was training again with my new unit to be sent as a replacement to the regiment in Russia, when one day, at the beginning of September 1942, I heard the army was looking for people who could speak German or English. I reported as being able to speak German, and was sent to Padua, again for an exam. While waiting for the exam in the barracks in Padua, I observed the arrival of new recruits from Sicily. They were far away from home, and after a very long train journey were very tired and dirty. However, they all wanted to send word home that they had arrived and were OK. It was then I noticed that they all huddled around one person, who sat at a table writing postcards. When I saw that each one of those recruits handed him a piece of paper, I realized they were unable to read or write: before leaving home the priest or another person who could read and write had given each of them a slip of paper with their address on it, so they could have someone write home for them. Coming from Germany where eight years in school was compulsory, I was surprised that such a situation could even be possible.

I did not have to wait long before being tested. An officer handed me a German newspaper and said, "Read." Of course, it was only natural that I would read very fluently, having had all my education in German schools. Before I was through with the article, the officer stopped me and said, *"Sie sprechen aber sehr gut Deutsch"* (You speak German very well,) and this with a heavy accent. Of course, I passed this exam and was ordered to return to my regiment, so I could be transferred to a newly created Interpreter Company attached to the 81st Infantry Regiment in Rome.

I arrived in Rome on September 10, 1942. The purpose of this interpreter company was to train us as interpreters and to familiarize us with military terminology pertaining to all kinds of armament and the expressions in war bulletins in both languages. The captain in charge of this company's German unit (the other half of the company was for English speakers) interviewed us, one at the time, as we reported to him. To his dismay, he discovered that most of us who came from German-speaking countries, like Germany, Austria, Switzerland and Luxembourg, spoke German very well, but were not fluent in Italian. About half of the 150 soldiers of the company were Italians from Italy. Of course they were fluent in Italian, but had only limited knowledge of German! The captain solved the dilemma by splitting the company in two: one group was given an intensive Italian course; the other a German one. This worked out well. In our half of the company were Italians from Switzerland, Germany, Austria and Luxembourg. One of those in the Italian half of the company was a Marchese Antinori, of the famous Florentine family now known worldwide for their Chianti wine.

So from September 10, 1942 to March 12, 1943, we received Italian lessons from officers who were university professors. During that time we had no military training whatsoever. I never fired a single shot with my rifle and I never cleaned it. Unfortunately, even though our barracks were in impressive buildings on Viale Giulio Cesare, they were not very clean. We were infested with lice. There were no showers. There wasn't even a room or a hall where we could eat. Once a day we stood in line in the inner courtyard to fetch our meal ration, which consisted of an indefinable substance, but on Sunday we did get *pasta-asciuta*. With our daily meal we were also given a hunk of bread, which we had to save for next morning's breakfast, hoping that nobody would steal it overnight. Since we were bunked in groups of four, when the trumpet sounded the morning wake up call, three of us could stay in bed a little longer, while the fourth, on alternating duty, went to the kitchen and brought up the big "marmites," along with a concoction still called coffee, and distributed it amongst us. We consumed this stuff with the chunk of bread we had saved from the day before – if we still had it. When we got to the bottom of the "marmite" one morning, we noticed a big dark lump, which turned out to be a cooked rat. Of course the officers and the non-commissioned officers ate in the officers' mess, a place we never saw, where they ate good civilian food prepared by good civilian chefs. That was the Italian Army at that time in that place.

Only once was there an alarm in the middle of the night; we had to go on alert, waiting in the yard for further orders. This lasted the whole night. The next morning we learned that the Americans had landed in Africa near Casablanca. That was in November 1942.

Life in Rome was quiet for me: I had no money! I had finally spent all the Marks I had saved and sent to Italy, and our pay did not make up for it. Actually, our pay was called the *decade*, because it was paid every ten days. My pay as a simple private was about thirteen Lire for ten days. With this amount I could not do much: I could buy a package of ten cigarettes, called *Milite*, for two Lire, a quart of wine for two Lire, a piece of bread for one Lira and one etto of olives (100 grams) for one Lira. This meant that almost twice every ten days I could afford that luxury, but I could not invite a girl to the movies nor go out to a café. On the other hand, there was no admission fee for all the museums and art galleries, the Vatican museums, or the churches with all their art treasures, and I made good use of those opportunities. It was there that I learned instinctively about composition and the visual arts, or must have, because when I started photography all my first images were well composed. When I saved enough money to go to a movie once in a while, I noticed the people always moved away from me. Later I found out that because I was a soldier in uniform the people were afraid they would pick up lice from me.

One day while I was in Rome I received a letter from San Lorenzello, near Benevento. It was in an unknown handwriting, with a sender by the name of Elisa Redivo. I could not imagine who that could be, but reading her letter and looking at the passport-type photo she included, I understood who she was – a cousin of mine who had never lived in Germany, although her family lived there in Rüdesheim. Her father was Angelo Redivo, a half-brother of my father, who died in 1929 when I was only ten years old. In her letter, Elisa invited me to spend a furlough with her. It was a very welcome invitation. I had been envying those of my comrades who could go on leave because they lived in Italy, which I couldn't because my parents lived in Germany. I got my leave and went to visit my cousin. She was not married, worked and lived in the house of a lawyer's family, and looked after the household. She was very kind to me, and so were the couple in whose house I was a guest. My visit with Elisa was a happy but completely unexpected experience, which enriched my life at a time I needed some support and affection. Afterwards I kept in touch with Elisa and was very sad when, while in the Prisoner of War camp in Algeria, I received a letter from the lawyer stating that Elisa was killed in the house by shrapnel during the advance of the Allies through that area.

During my time in Rome, I was a rather lonely and somewhat homesick young man. I craved some outside social contact, but did not know anyone in Rome. After a while, I thought of looking in the telephone book to see if there were any Redivos listed. It so happened there were – only two Redivos for a population of two million people! I dared myself to phone them, to find out if they had any connection with my family, or with the village of Roveredo. The first Redivo I phoned had come to Rome from Trieste, although his ancestors had come from Roveredo many years back, but the other one, Dionisio Redivo, was from Roveredo. He had a construction contracting business with his sons in Rome. When I identified myself, he invited me to visit him at his home. My visit proved very rewarding: it turned out that before the First World War my father had him come from Roveredo to Wiesbaden to work for him. He said he remembered and respected my father very much, and that my father paid well and promptly. He also commented on my mother, saying that she was a beautiful woman and very kind. Of course, I was happy to hear these favourable comments about my parents. I received a standing invitation to come and visit whenever I wanted, and the Dionisio Redivo family became a home away from home for me. The children of the family were like brothers and sisters to me, and with them I found the home I was looking for. This made my life much easier and my poverty more bearable. They did not give me any money, but from time to time I could eat a good Italian meal in good company and a welcoming family atmosphere.

After six months of studying the language, the time had come for exams, both written and oral. It was announced that the ten best would be immediately assigned to posts in headquarters where interpreters were needed – this could be anywhere in Russia or North Africa where Italian and German troops were fighting side by side. It so happened that I was one of those ten. We also were told that steps were being taken to promote us to the rank of second lieutenant. Unfortunately, this proposal never worked its way through the military bureaucracy in time to reach me before I became a Prisoner of War.

While I was in Rome, the city was full of German soldiers, and with them were uniformed young women called *Blitzmädel* (Blitz Girls), who were office staff or communication aides. One day just before I was transferred from Rome, I made the acquaintance of one of them, Anneliese, a girl from Rottweil. We had a few dates, during which we went on walks in the Villa Borghese, a big park in the middle of Rome. One time, we kissed good night when she walked me back to my barracks. Incredibly, at that same moment the military police patrol, *La Ronda*, came by, a group of three soldiers who made the rounds through the city to see that no soldier was making trouble or was illegally out on the town. When they saw me kiss Anneliese, they arrested me and took me to my barracks, which wasn't very far away. The girl was stunned and scared, but could do nothing to help me. I spent the night in the barracks jail for kissing my girl in public, which was considered unbecoming behaviour for a soldier. When I appeared the next morning in front of the captain commanding the company, he asked me why I had spent the night in the jail. When I explained to him exactly what had happened, he dismissed me with a smile and said, "Next time, don't get caught!"

Anneliese and I got along very well; it was a truly platonic love, short as it was. On the 12th of March 1943, I received my orders to report to the 30th Army Corps Headquarters in Tunisia. When I had to leave by train for Sicily and then Tunisia, I asked Anneliese to see me off at the train station, but she said she was on duty at that time and that it would be impossible. So we said good-bye. But when the day came and I was on the platform at the train station, she came running towards me and we had a few minutes together before I had to mount the train and wave good-bye from the window. That was the last time I saw or heard from her. She said she had asked permission from her boss to see me off, who was none other than Field Marshall Kesselring, the commander of all the German troops in the Italian Theatre of Operations. I never could get in touch with Anneliese again, but I preserved good memories.

To this I have to add that when I knew that I was to be transferred to Tunisia I wrote to my parents in a cynical way: "From now on watch the progress of events in North Africa, where I am going. Surely great changes will now take place there!" And after I was there for two months, they surely did, because that was the end of the Axis campaign in North Africa. The Afrika Korps, which was no longer under Rommel, was driven from Libya all the way to Tunisia by the British Eighth Army under Montgomery, and on May 14, 1943 General Hans-Jürgen von Arnim, who had taken over the Afrika Korps, surrendered with 250,000 men to the Allied Forces under General Eisenhower, including all the Italian Forces under General Messe, which included me.

6. *Spies in Kairouan*

To get to Africa, I traveled alone by train to Castelvetrano, in the southwest corner of Sicily, from where I would be flown to Tunis. For me, the trip was very memorable: the crossing of the Strait of Messina, from Reggio Calabria to Messina, was the first time I had ever travelled on a big ship on the sea. It was a calm crossing.

On arrival in the port of Messina there were many fruit venders. Their main products were ripe blood oranges, of a ripeness and juicy sweetness I had never experienced before, nor had ever imagined could exist. From Messina, a train brought me to Castelvetrano, where I reported to the military airport authorities. At the airport, there were other military personnel to be flown to Tunisia. We were about to be loaded into the airplane when the pilot of the plane, an old beat up Savoia transport with lots of bullet holes in the fuselage, came to tell us that he was not flying that day: he did not feel right and he would surely be shot down. He said he would fly the next day instead. Apparently his superiors respected his wish and we did not fly. We were assigned to some improvised accommodation to spend the night.

Since the evening was free and I had a few Lire left, I decided to go to the movies. When I stood at the wicket to buy my ticket from the pretty girl who sold them, I started a conversation with her. Since there was no one else around at the moment we chatted for a few minutes. Then suddenly I felt some pointed object being pressed into my back, and a male voice ordered me to shut up and leave instantly and not try to talk to the girl again, or else. Knowing that I was in Sicily, where by reputation such threats were not made idly, I obeyed, and disappeared into the cinema without looking back.

Back at the airport on the next day, we climbed into this old airplane and took off for Tunisia. Before we departed, the pilot told us that he would fly very low over the water to avoid enemy interception and that when he landed the plane we had to get out immediately and run as fast as we could away from it, because the British would probably sweep down on the airfield to try to destroy any planes that touched down. That's exactly how it happened: he flew low over the water without incident, and after landing we got out and ran; as soon as we had gotten away from the plane the Spitfires came and strafed the airfield. I did not see if they got the plane.

By this time it was late, and I had no transportation to proceed to Hammamet, where the Headquarters of the 30th Army Corps was located. Tunis was a big city, with a large Italian population: one of the soldiers who was with me on the plane said he knew a family nearby who would be willing to put us up for the night. I agreed to go with him, and we went there, ate some good Tunisian food, and slept on the floor. For a pillow, I used my artillery roll – a kind of duffel bag – containing all my spare clothes, including my shoes, some letters and other mementos. When I woke up in the morning it was gone. I had not noticed it being taken from under my head. There were several other solders in the house overnight and the owners had young sons, but no one knew anything about my duffel bag or who might have taken it. One of the other soldiers had his wristwatch stolen, or so he claimed. There was nothing I could do, except to proceed to my headquarters and report the incident. In a way it was nice to be without the burden of this stuff. The lost clothing and shoes were never replaced. I wore my one remaining set of things continuously for three months, until, as a Prisoner of War I received new outfits from the American Army.

At the 30th Army Corps Headquarters I was assigned to a Captain of the Granatieri who was the liaison officer for his headquarters and the German Headquarters in Kairouan, the command post for the defence of the western border of Tunisia. There the attack by the Americans was concentrated, who had landed in Casablanca in November 1942 and had fought their way through the Kasserin Mountains in Tunisia. The German commanding officer was a colonel and did not like Italians at all, while my captain, who did not like Germans, avoided all encounters with the German colonel. Because I spoke fluent German, the German colonel wanted me to transfer to the German Army. He said, "Take off those Italian rags and I'll give you a proper uniform, and you can stay with us." I had certainly no inclination to accept that offer, but in that tense situation I had to decline very diplomatically.

Because the Italian Captain and the German Colonel disliked each other, when I had to translate conversations between them I was often put in frustrating, even dangerous situations. They would mix insults into their sentences, which I could never translate literally without the risk of serious consequences. Sometimes I felt that by rephrasing and formulating their utterances against each other I was carrying on a conversation with myself. Fortunately, that situation lasted only a few weeks. Another strange part of that time was that my captain would often send me alone to the German Headquarters to obtain a report about the daily position of the front. On these occasions, the German colonel would tell me one thing, while I could see on the big map that the pins were on different spots from what he was telling me.

The most important thing that happened while I was in Kairouan was an assignment to accompany two Arab spies to the front line, which at that moment was at Pichon, about fifty or sixty kilometres to the west. There were only German troops in that whole sector of the front. The job of the two spies was to go over to the other side behind the British lines and then return to report their strength and positions back to us. The spies had agreed to receive half of their fee before going and the other half after they reported back. Along with those two Arabs, I hitched a ride with a German courier in a jeep-type vehicle, a *Wüstenkübel*, an air-cooled, modified Volkswagen. At the edge of the front line, where the German infantry was in position and where the driver's destination diverged from our own, the two Arabs and I got off. We walked the rest of the way on foot. When we came to a German guard post, the guard called out for a password, which I did not know. The guard was about to shoot us, when I shouted to him in German to first let me talk to him and to listen to what I had to say. He agreed, but insisted he must first shoot the two Arabs, because no civilian was allowed in this area. Again I pleaded with him and explained the purpose of their being here with me. I must have pleaded well, because he accepted and trusted me. As we talked further and I got to hear his dialect better, I concluded that he came from the same part of the Rheinland as I did. When I introduced myself, he told me that he knew my father, who had done some work for his father. After that, he showed us where the minefields were and how to get to where we wanted to go, and where the two Arabs could most safely cross the line. It was growing dark, the front was completely quiet, and we reached our destination without incident. There we met an Italian lieutenant, who was the liaison officer in that sector of the front, although there were no Italian troops. We bedded down in the field for the night, while the Arabs started to walk off towards the spot where they would cross over. The night was quiet, with a bright moon.

7. Eighty Cents per Day

At dawn, we were awoken by artillery. The British, who opposed us in that sector, had decided to attack. Soon we heard the grinding of heavy tank tracks in the distance. Those noises came closer and louder. The men of the German infantry company that held that section of the front were lying on the ground behind some protective piled-up soil, with their rifles at the ready. From some soldiers who were retreating from an advanced position, we learned that all the anti-tank guns had been overrun and that the front was in retreat. On hearing this, the captain in command of this company gave orders to retreat, because the odds for his small company of infantry to hold up the big British tanks were as good as impossible. Because of the situation, we three Italians – the lieutenant, his orderly and I – were, so to speak, also under the command of this German captain. The grinding noise of the British tanks was on us almost immediately. They ground ahead steadily without encountering any resistance and were followed by infantrymen who where shooting at us. The Germans were in full retreat and did not shoot back. Everybody was running back under the fire of the tanks and the infantrymen. I have never forgotten seeing a British soldier, beside a moving tank about a hundred metres away, wearing his flat helmet, with his rifle at his shoulder, aiming right at me and shooting. I began running at full speed, zigzagging and ducking behind structures and trees. The Italian lieutenant had given me his backpack to carry, but it was too heavy, and because I was running for my life I just dropped it and kept running. Because of my mission with the two Arabs I had no rifle, but I did have two hand grenades. I was never trained to fire or throw one, though, so while running I just threw them away. Despite all that shooting I did not see any of the Germans or Italians being hit, probably because we were all so spread out and therefore not easy targets. There was one stretch of the land that went slightly uphill. It was a big field of mustard in bloom like a big yellow carpet. As I ran through it, I heard bullets whistling by my head and body. After crossing that mustard field, I reached the crest of the hill. The terrain went down on the other side. I was out of sight of the enemy's tanks and soldiers there, but I kept right on running with the lieutenant's orderly, a fellow from Luxembourg. The lieutenant was well behind us, but eventually, when we could slow down, we met again. That is when we heard the noise of German tanks coming towards us to engage the British tanks in battle.

We still had to walk about seventeen kilometres before we were back in Kairouan. We arrived safely but very exhausted. I can't forget the brief conversation I had with one of the German tank commanders. Standing in and looking down from the tower of his enormous Tiger tank, he said that he greatly admired the Italian tank troops who sat in tin boxes (coffee grinders he called them), which they called tanks, and went on the attack against the strong and powerful American and British Sherman tanks. He thought they were real heroes. This was good to hear, since the Italian soldiers were always ridiculed and belittled by their German allies, but, still, a dead Italian soldier is just as dead as a German one. If the Italian soldiers were not being sacrificed unnecessarily, it was because a live soldier was worth far more to his unit than a dead one.

On our return to Kairouan, our small contingent of liaison personnel received orders to return to headquarters in Hamamet, because the Allies had broken through the line of defense in our sector and were about to take Kairouan. This was in the beginning of May 1943, and the war in North Africa was drawing to its end. Our headquarters unit had received orders to return to Rome and to evacuate on boats sent to us on the peninsula of Cape Bone. We gathered near the shore and the designated landing site. While I was waiting there, squadrons of B-27s dropped bombs over us. I was lying underneath some prickly pear cacti, when straight above me, not too high at all, about two dozen of those bombers opened their bomb bays and the bombs came falling out. You would think they were coming straight down to hit you, but they did not: they fell at least five or six kilometres beyond the place where we were hiding. The momentum of the planes gave them that forward shove to strike far ahead from where the bays were opened.

Then we received news that the boats that were supposed to pick us up and take us back to Italy had all been sunk before they could reach the point

assigned for our embarkation. With that, it became clear that we would become Prisoners of War. At this point our captain (the one for whom I was
interpreter) gave orders to hide out in an *Uvadi* (a gully) near the coastal
highway and wait. We still had a truck with lots of food parked at the edge
of the road at the entrance to the Uvadi. While waiting there, we heard of
the surrender of the Italian and German Forces. The war in North Africa
was over. The captain gave orders to destroy our weapons, mostly old rifles
and the odd handgun the non-commissioned officers carried. When I
smashed my old rifle, out of which I had never fired a shot and which I had
never cleaned, I actually felt quite relieved that I could throw it away. We
just stayed in this gulley, waiting for something to happen. Two men were
sent daily to the truck to get food. Around this time our captain also gave us
orders to bring as much of the food as possible up into the gulley and then
to burn the truck so that it would not fall into enemy hands. This time it was
my turn to go to the truck with another soldier. There was no traffic on the
highway.

As we started to pour out some gasoline, with the intention of burning
the truck, a single motorcycle came along the highway and stopped. A soldier
in khaki uniform and shorts got off and strolled towards us, with his hands in
his pockets. He asked us in good Italian what we were doing there. We answered that we wanted to burn the truck so that the enemy wouldn't get it.
Then he said, "I wouldn't do that because you might have to walk a long way
to the next Prisoner of War camp." It was at this moment that we realized this
soldier was a British soldier who spoke fluent Italian. As it turned out, he came
from the Island of Malta, where they speak both English and Italian. He asked
how many we were and if we had an officer with us. We told him we were
about forty men with one captain. He said that one of us should go and get the
captain, while the other should stay with him. That is what we did. When the
captain met this soldier (who might have been a sergeant), he made the gesture of surrendering by wanting to hand over his officer's pistol, a Beretta,
but the British soldier said, "No, you keep it. Have you still any ammunition
for it?" When the captain said no, the soldier reached in his pocket and with-
drew a handful of shells, asking, "Will these fit? You will need some to defend

yourselves from the marauding Arabs who are taking advantage of the confusion and are robbing disarmed soldiers during the night. Tomorrow morning, you can get on your truck and just drive west. Military Police are on all
intersections of roads to direct you to the nearest POW Camp." That's how I
became a Prisoner of War at Kelibia, Tunisia. It was May 11, 1943. My predic-
tion to my parents, that major events would take place in Afrika after my arrival there had proved correct.

Our group of forty was the Intelligence Unit of the 30th Army Corps Headquarters. We had the safe with all the codebooks, containing the keys for de-
ciphering coded military communications. When it was clear that we would
be captured, our captain gave orders to destroy everything that was in the safe.
I was one of those assigned to do that. Among the items in the safe was a thick
Italian-English and English-Italian dictionary, a Spinelli. When I saw this I
decided not to burn it, but to keep it, in light of the fact that in a short time I
would be a Prisoner of War of either the British or the Americans, and I would
be better off if I learned English as fast as possible. I tore the dictionary in two
halves and put one half in my left and the other in the right pocket of my jacket.
It was a smart move.

There was a sergeant in our group who was very distraught and upset
when he realized he would become a prisoner. He cried and carried on in the
most desperate manner. He was afraid the Negroes of the American Army
would torture him and probably even kill him. He was terrified, and it was
hard to quiet him down. I personally had no concerns about becoming a Prisoner of War, and seeing someone else so helpless gave me the strength to comfort him and others. Of course, by doing so I instilled confidence and security
in myself too. As it turned out, when we drove along the highway the next day
in the direction of the Prisoner of War camp at Constantine – near the Algerian border – we ran out of gas and stopped on the side of the highway. The
first truck coming towards us was full of American soldiers, all Negroes. They
stopped, jumped off their truck and came running towards us, handing out
chewing gum and asking for souvenirs. After this first major encounter with
the victorious enemy, everyone was relieved, and we knew we would be safe
and in good hands.

While driving from Cape Bone through the countryside to Constantine we knew why the Allies, especially the Americans, had won the African Campaign, and knew as well that they would win the war: for miles and miles along the roads were stockpiles of vehicles, tanks, guns, ammunition, piles of food and gasoline stores. It never ended. We could not believe our eyes that so much material could be brought over the Atlantic despite the sinking of so many ships by U-boats. Those 10,000-ton liberty ships, built by Kaiser, had done it.

The first Prisoner of War camp, Chancy, near Constantine, was Camp #127. We stayed there for three weeks. It was only a transition camp, run by the British. In one swoop the Allies had taken 250,000 German and Italian Prisoners of War. These were the remnant of Rommel's Africa Korps under General von Arnim. General Messe was the Commander of the Italian Forces in Africa. Both of them had surrendered, along with their troops. Suddenly the Allies, who weren't prepared for it, had to feed, shelter and guard us all. The three weeks I stayed in that transition camp, plus a three-day train ride from Constantine to Oran, were the worst I have ever experienced. The camp was so crowded that most of us had to sleep on gravel in the open. There must have been between four and five thousand soldiers in a camp that could really accommodate only a few hundred, in one large and several smaller tents. At night it was freezing cold, while by day it was boiling hot, without shade or water. We were divided into "Centurions," units of a hundred. Each group received ten small tins of corned beef (from Argentina), a few Graham wafers, and lots of tea. The toilet conditions were unbearable, with overflowing barrels and then a big mess spreading further and further out around them. I stayed three long weeks in that camp, with conditions growing worse every day. Understandably, the British had neither the food nor the facilities to look after so many people, yet they couldn't just let us loose into the countryside, either – after all we were a beaten enemy force. Each day, some guards came to the gate to collect between eighty to a hundred people to work for them in their field quarters and kitchen. Those fortunate enough to be picked received enough to eat on that day and could clean themselves a little. On one morning I was lucky enough to be picked, and got out with a rather large contingent.

Instead of going to the British quarters and kitchens, however, we were loaded into the cattle cars of a train, with French-Arab guards. After waiting for hours, the train started moving. No one knew where it would take us. We travelled for three days and two nights, stopping once in a while, and without getting out of the cattle cars for either toilets or water. We received no food and only once was some water handed in. We were about forty people to a car. The smell was indescribable. I did my business in my cap and threw it out of a narrow open slot on the side of the car. One urinated through the cracks in the floor. It was an unforgettable experience. After having survived an ordeal, one often says: "I wouldn't want to have missed it." Not in this case, although it was educational – if you lived through it. On the other hand, later on I considered myself rather lucky to have been on the train that took me to an American Prisoner of War camp, rather than on another one that took some Italian Prisoners of War to French camps in the Sahara Desert, subjected to French-Arab guards. Later, some of those who came back from those camps looked starved, and claimed to have been mistreated. Some alleged to have had the gold fillings removed from their teeth with the guard's bayonets, and told of other atrocities as well.

When we finally arrived at a small railroad station, near St. Barbe du Tletate, about forty-five kilometres south of Oran, a large detail of American soldiers with their rifles on their hips received us. They organized us into columns, then under a burning sun and through deep dust marched us for about five or six miles to our holding camp: Camp #131. Even though it was only a transition camp for German and Italian Prisoners of War, to hold them until they would be shipped to the States, it became my home for almost two full years. It was here that the guards wanted to take away my dictionary. After arriving at the camp, all prisoners were searched. Valuables like money, cameras, watches and books were taken away for storage in envelopes marked with prisoners' names and POW identification numbers. My number was 81-I-32894. When a guard tried to take away my English-Italian dictionary, I screamed at the top of my voice, in Italian: "Help, he wants to take away my dictionary! I need it to learn English!" First, the Italian-speaking sergeant, who supervised the processing of the POW's, wanted to shut me up and take the two dictionary halves away. But fortunately the Captain in charge of the whole operation heard the confusion and came to see what was the matter. When I explained that the reason I wanted to have the dictionaries was to learn English as quickly as possible, to possibly be of use to them, because I speak German besides Italian, he said, "Let him have his dictionary." I still have the two halves.

After the search, we were sent to showers and delousing. We were terribly thirsty after that long inhuman train ride and the grueling march through heat and dust. When we were finally in our assigned stockades, our guards brought a water truck outside our stockade. We all hoped we would finally be given water, but the German-speaking corporal (I found out later he was a Jew from Vienna) who was supposed to give us water, opened the tap instead and let all the water run out while watching us with a big grin on his face. We remained thirsty. As we learned in time, when the commanding officer of the camp, a major, heard about it, he reprimanded the corporal. Although I considered it inhumane, when I remembered the treatment of the Jews in Germany I could understand why. I did not yet know about the extermination camps.

As we settled in to our stockade, the Americans asked for volunteers for the kitchen – people with trades such as cooks and bakers. Because I was a baker (and lucky, too!) I was chosen to work in the kitchen. The camp was a big camp, with twelve stockades, as they were called, separated by barbed wire. The entire complex itself was double-fenced. Each stockade held three thousand Prisoners of War. In eight of them were German prisoners; the other four held Italian prisoners. Outside these compounds was also a hospital, in tents, run by German prisoner personnel. The camp was guarded from towers in the corners of each stockade, with machine-gun equipped guards. Each stockade was divided in two parts – a smaller section was for the kitchen and the camp office, and a larger section held the tents for the three thousand men. At the top end of the camp were the rows of latrines.

Being in the kitchen gave me daily contact with the American supply sergeant, who spoke only English. None of the other kitchen staff spoke any English. The sergeant gave orders in English and sign language. Having my dictionary, which contained also some English grammar, rules and usage, and with my German background, I had a good foundation for learning English. Also, every week the supply sergeant brought me the Stars and Stripes army newspaper to read, so I learned quickly and was well informed of what was going on in the world. I helped my English along in my free hours as well, by trying to talk to the guards on the towers. One of them gave me a pipe to hold between my teeth to improve my pronunciation, which I did. It worked, producing an American-English accent!

During the time when I worked in the kitchen, I hoped to be transported to the United States. When I asked Captain Rainwater how to go about it, he understood my desire to go to the States right away, and suggested I should declare myself a Fascist: then I would probably be sent there immediately. This did not sound like good advice, so I checked it with another American officer, Lieutenant Powers, who said, "Don't you do that!" When I said that Captain Rainwater had suggested it, Lieutenant Powers told me that Captain Rainwater was being discharged from the Army because of mental illness and was being sent home.

One day, the Camp Commander came to inspect our stockade's kitchen. The supply sergeant, with whom I could by now converse quite well, called me to interpret for the Commander, who wanted to talk with the kitchen's Italian chef. When the Commander heard how well I spoke English, he said to the sergeant, "How come you keep this man in the kitchen? He is of much greater use up in the headquarters, especially since he is also fluent in German."

The next day I moved out of camp into a special open compound near the headquarters offices and started working there together with about twenty or so GI's. I was given my own desk, filing cabinet and Underwood typewriter, like all the American staff of that office. My job was to keep the records of each Prisoner of War in the camp. Each one had a file card with his vital statistics, finger prints and photograph. Prisoners either arrived from another camp with these records, or they were processed in this camp. Whenever an empty Liberty ship was available, prisoners were shipped to the States. From then on I was part of the ISU 7004 Prisoner of War Administration Company of the United States Army in Africa, a position I held until January 18, 1945. On that date we left Africa to be transferred to Livorno, Italy, where I continued to work in the American Headquarters office until my release from custody of the U.S. Army.

I should not omit to mention that after Mussolini's fall in September 1943, Maresciallo Badoglio was invited by the King to head a new Italian government, which signed an armistice with the Allies and distanced itself from Hitler and Germany. Generals of the new Italian Army, now under Badoglio's command, came to our camp to ask us Italian Prisoners of War if we wanted to remain true to our oath of allegiance to the King and therefore to the new government, or if we wanted to continue our allegiance to Mussolini. By then Mussolini had been rescued from his exile on Monte Sasso and had declared an Italian republic in northern Italy, *La Repubblica di Salò*. That part of northern Italy was now under German occupation. Out of the three thousand men, only three wanted to continue to support Mussolini and his new republic. One of them was actually a friend of mine, although I never shared his political views. From then on, the rest of us were designated collaborators and cobelligerents; no more Italian Prisoners of War were shipped to the States. In keeping with the Geneva Convention, we received pay of ten cents U.S. per day; if we worked, we received an additional eighty cents per day. A crew of selected Italian office workers kept track of these payments and wrote payrolls for thousands of Italian and German Prisoners of War.

8. Swimming With the GI's

Once we had become "collaborators," life in camp became comfortable. Every ten days we received so-called "luxuries," which consisted of Bull Durham tobacco with cigarette paper, a bar of soap, toothpaste, shaving cream, razors and razor blades, pencils and form letters on which to write home, and sometimes even Algerian wine. We had everything, except we could not go out on a date. Once a month I enjoyed the privilege of watching a movie with the GI's. As a whole it was an uneventful time, with the exception of the odd incident. In the German stockades some killings took place. In 1943, any German Prisoner of War who said he did not approve of Hitler any more and that Germany would lose the war, was in great danger from his fellow prisoners. At times, such actions resulted in soldiers being found dead in the latrines. Whenever a German soldier was missing at roll call, the first place the Americans looked was in the latrines. The culprits were never found, and after the whole stockade was punished with smaller rations and denied "luxuries," life would go on as usual. Still, such events were unusual. People learned to keep their mouths shut.

One day, a huge cloud suddenly darkened the sky in the middle of the day. Soon it started "raining" – not water but locusts. They hit the tents like hail. It sounded exactly the same. It was a repulsive experience to walk through the camp and to feel and hear the insects crunching underfoot. They were so dense one could not avoid stepping on them. After I saw that, I found it easy to understand the description in the Bible about this plague.

On another occasion we were taken to the Mediterranean coast for a swim, sixty-five kilometres northeast of Oran. About ten trucks brought us to the beach, driven by Italian POW's. Each truck was loaded with forty to forty-five men and maybe five American GI's. They weren't there to guard us, though, because nobody would want to run away: we had nowhere to go, especially anywhere where we would be treated as well and with such a good life as we had in the camp.

My work time in the office was relaxed and I received cigarettes and chewing gum from privates, corporals, T-sergeants and even staff sergeants. The commanding officer in charge of these Headquarters of the 7004th Prisoner of War Administration Company (OVHD) U.S. Army, APO 600, was a major. His adjutant was 1st Lieutenant Infantry, Peter C. Casperson. At the end of my service at this headquarters, Lieutenant Casperson gave me a letter of reference and a recommendation, "To whom it may Concern," with this text:

1. Sold. Ugo Redivo, 81-I-32894, has worked for over a year in this headquarters as an interpreter and as a personnel clerk for both the German and Italian sections. He has performed all duties in a superior manner and I recommend him highly for this type of work.

2. He speaks German, Italian and English fluently and also has a good knowledge of French.

Signed: PETER C. CASPERSON,
1st Lt., Infantry, Adjutant

While I was still working in the kitchen, one of my comrades, Egone Bonini, who came from Bolzano, gave me a big book, a German Brockhaus Encyclopaedia. Egone was the attendant for Captain Rainwater, who spoke German – his name had originally been Regenwasser, before being literally translated into English. Egone gave me the encyclopaedia because he knew I spoke German and that I would enjoy having it. I did not ask where he got it from and put it on a shelf in the staff room in the kitchen. One day Captain Rainwater came into the kitchen for an inspection. While roaming around, he saw my encyclopaedia on the shelf. He picked it up, looked at it, asked whose it was and then said: "Look at that, I have one just like it in my tent." I thought nothing of it, but the next time I saw Egone I asked him where he had found the encyclopaedia. He answered that he had found it in Captain Rainwater's tent. Well, I did not worry too much about the Captain's comment. Nothing happened, and I still have the book here in Canada. I have no idea how I ever brought such a big book all the way from that Prisoner of War camp in Africa to my new country.

As mentioned, once I left the kitchen I kept the records and files of all the German and Italian POW's. Whenever a Liberty ship was returning empty to the United States, Lieutenant Casperson would say to me, "Hugo, give me the files of three hundred or six hundred (or whatever number) of German POW's." The Liberty ships were 10,000-ton freighters, mass-produced by the automaker Kaiser in California to bring war supplies to the European Theatre of Operations. They were made with steel plates welded together instead of riveted, a first in shipbuilding at that time. Of course, the procedure for choosing prisoners to be shipped back to the States was that the first to come to Camp #131 were the first to be shipped out. However, one day about five hundred new prisoners arrived in camp, who wore German uniforms but could not speak German. From their records I saw that they were all Russians, most of them from Azerbaijan, who the Germans had forced to fight around Monte Casino in Italy, where they were captured. They had just arrived, and because of those absolutely strange and unfamiliar names I filed their records with great difficulty. One day shortly after that, Lieutenant Casperson asked me to give him five hundred "Jerries" (the standard nickname for Germans) for shipment to the States. I decided to "get rid of the Russians," and gave their records to the personnel in charge, who took these prisoners to the port of Oran. My life had been going along quite comfortably, and I did not want to be saddled with those strange, and difficult, names and records! Only two or three of these people spoke any German.

All went fine and I was relieved not to have to cope with the Russian names any longer, but about a month later Lieutenant Casperson came out of his office looking straight at me and waving his index finger, with a stern expression on his face. In his other hand he held a copy of TIME magazine, which he was waving at me. It turned out that the media had found out about those Russians in German uniforms arriving in the States as Prisoners of War, and the politicians were questioning why they had not been sent back to Russia. Apparently, the "error" was traced right back to Lieutenant Casperson's desk, and he was held responsible. However, the case had no serious consequences and the scolding I got, after I explained the reason why I had done it, was not too severe. Maybe I saved some lives, because we also learned that all Russians who became Prisoners of War of the Germans were severely punished, or even executed, if and when they arrived back in Russia.

Because of the daily contact I had with the Americans in the office, I decided to immigrate to the U.S. after the war. This desire became even stronger when I saw the way these men of different ranks treated each other, in comparison with the difference in rank in the Italian Army, and even more so in the German Army, where all was rank and discipline. I need to give only one example. The American corporal who was sitting at the switchboard, leaning back in his chair, with his feet up, stayed exactly in that position when the major, the camp's Commanding Officer, came into the office in the morning. The major would walk in with a cigar in his mouth and would say, "Good morning, Joe," and Joe would say, "Good morning, Major." Of course, we others would also stay in our places, the way we were, and would say, "Good morning, Major." The same scene in a German headquarters office would be very different: the corporal, as well as everyone else under the rank of major, would jump up, stand at attention, salute and not move until the major gave the command to be at ease. In the Italian Army it wouldn't be quite as formal, but still more formal.

I recall one funny exchange with Lieutenant Casperson, when he casually asked me, "Well, Hugo, if there should be a war between the Russians and the Americans, on whose side would you fight?" Without hesitation and in all seriousness I replied, "On the Russian side, of course!" He did not expect this reply and was very surprised, but before he could ask me why, I explained. "I would prefer to become a Prisoner of War of the Americans again," I told him, "and not fall into the hands of the Russians!" Lieutenant Casperson had a good laugh about this backhanded compliment of my treatment as a Prisoner of War. In fact, the treatment was very good. Even now when I mention to Americans that I was a Prisoner of War of the U.S. Army for two years, I get compassionate looks and comments. People are always surprised when I say that up to then those were the best years of my life: I was free of stress, safe from the war, well looked after, had food and shelter, a good job which I liked because I could learn English and improve my typing skills at my leisure, and all this in pleasant surroundings and good company in the form of the American personnel and my Italian comrades.

The offices were in a large farmhouse with a big yard and garden in which the tents of the office staff were located. When asked later about how we were treated by the Americans, I usually answered, "We had everything, except girls." Moreover, I believe they looked after this part of our lives by putting something in our food – it was said to be soda – that would curb our normal urges, although once I was approached in an amorous way by one of the men who slept in our tent. There were eight of us in each tent, sleeping on improvised beds made of two-by-fours with blankets stretched tightly across as mattresses. The sleeping was arranged with head and feet in one bed and feet and head in the other. Of course I refused this man's advances and reported the incident to the American T-Sergeant, Victor Barret, who was in the little tent-office in our stockade. Without making any fuss, he gave the man a warning and transferred him to another tent. Actually, that was the only time I was aware that such a thing might happen in a camp with only men. I was aware of no other cases.

In my tent was also a Prince, Principe Pignatelli, whom I saw later quite by coincidence in Rome in 1946. He was supposed to be an officer and therefore in the officers' camp, but when he became a Prisoner of War he had not yet received his commission, so he remained with us. The officers were in the camp next to ours, but because each man had to look after his own hygiene and had to wash his own clothes, it turned out that we, the rank and file, were much cleaner than the officers. The Americans also observed this and did not think very much of the way the officers looked after themselves. Of course, before the officers were POW's their attendants did all their washing and looked after their every need.

In this camp I befriended T-Sergeant Victor Barret, who spoke German and was in charge of our stockade, Stockade #3 of camp 131. I got along very well with him and mentioned that I would like to immigrate to the U.S. after the war. Unlike Captain Rainwater, he offered to provide me with an affidavit of support, which I would need if I made an application for an immigration visa at an American consulate after the war. This he actually did, but the story of that comes later.

9. *Gioia*

By January 1945, the Allies had fought their way up the Italian boot above Bologna, and had freed Italy to the south of there from the Germans. On January 19, 1945, the Italian Prisoners of War, now Allied Collaborators, were transferred to Camp #180, a tent city in Oran, and on January 23, 1945 embarked on the British passenger ship *Eastern Prince*, which had been converted to a troop transport. On January 28, 1945, we disembarked at Naples. It was a long journey, because we made calls on different ports, for reasons I don't know. We slept in hammocks. Our spirits were up, because we were moving towards home, but a little fearful at the same time, because there was the danger of being sunk by a German U-boat. But nothing happened, or I would not be writing this story!

After a few days in a transition camp in Puzzuoli, near Naples, I was again picked out of the crowd, and was sent to Livorno (Leghorn) to join S-2, the Intelligence Section of the 2694th Technical Supervision Regiment (OVHD), APO 782, of the US Army, under Captain J. De Stafano, Infantry. Still a Prisoner of War, I was now wearing the GI's regular khaki uniform. The only thing that distinguished me from the American soldiers was an insignia in the form of the geographical boot of Italy, sewn to the upper left arm on my shirtsleeve. As was standard for other military personnel, I was accommodated in a bombed-out private house in the city. Our various headquarters were located in big undamaged government buildings. I was free to move about the city, where, very slowly, civilians were moving back from the countryside to the houses (if they were still standing) from which they had fled during the bombing and the fighting.

It was a very interesting time for me. The Americans I worked with asked me to give them Italian language lessons, which I did. To make contact with the civilian population, I decided to go to the only protestant church in the city. It was not damaged. There I met a German-speaking lady, Mrs. Santarini, who was of Swiss origin. The church was a Chiesa Valdese, a Protestant congregation originating in northwestern Italy. The lady kindly invited me to her home to meet her family. Of course, after almost two years in a Prisoner of War camp I was happy to be a guest in a real family. Mr. Santarini was a high school teacher. They had two daughters, Franca and Gioia. Franca had a boy-friend, Toni, and Gioia was a chemistry student at the University of Pisa, about thirty kilometres north of Livorno. The Santarini family lived in an undam-aged house in Livorno, at number 6 Via dei Cavallegeri, which was near the sea on the way to Antignano and Calafuria, a rocky promontory along the Tirranian Coast.

This contact with an Italian family gave me the opportunity to start a friendship with their daughter, Gioia. Even though she spoke German excel-lently, we always communicated in Italian. She introduced me to Italian lit-erature and was well versed in German literature. Because I was interested in literature, we got along very well. Although I had not been in the company of girls for two years, ours remained a platonic love, because she was brought up as an Italian daughter, with high moral standards. Some of the fondest memo-ries of our times together were the hours we spent sunbathing on the rocky beach of Calafuria, while discussing all manners of topics and swimming in the Mediterranean. When it was stormy it was a challenge to get out of the water again, because the waves smashed against the rocks and you had to grip one of the outcroppings and hold on for dear life until the wave receded or the next wave came and put you up a little higher. This was in the summer of 1945.

In June 1947, my future wife, Dorothy, and I travelled from Switzerland to Italy for a holiday. On that occasion we visited Gioia and the Santarini fam-ily, but, sadly, Gioia was not at home. However, since we were very tired from an overnight train ride, with many delays and changing of trains with differ-ent connections, Mrs. Santarini suggested that Dorothy should lie on Gioia's bed to rest and sleep awhile. I found it especially amusing that my fiancée should sleep on the bed of my former girlfriend.

In the summer of 1970, I had another unusual encounter with Gioia's family. On a five-week trip to Europe with our two sons, Marcus and Selwyn, I wanted to show them were I used to go swimming with my girlfriend, so we stopped to do some sunbathing and swimming at Calafuria. While there, I told my sons about the lovely times I had spent with Gioia on this romantic spot along the sea. As I was in the middle of telling the story, I saw a woman with a child clinging to her hand climbing down the rocky wall and walking across a flat rock area towards us. When I caught a glimpse of her face, the words got stuck in my mouth and I said, "That is she!" My children must have thought, "Oh yes, the 'Old Man' sees ghosts," because from the time of the story in 1945 to 1970, all of twenty-five years had passed, and I had seen her only once again, in 1968, when on a very brief visit in Milan. Anyway, I approached her, stopped in front of her, and all I could say was: "Gioia?" Well this lady with the child stopped, smiled at me, and said: *"No, sono la sorella Franca."* (No, I am her sister Franca.) It was not a ghost. I hadn't seen Franca since 1945, and at that time the two sisters did not at all look alike, but after twenty-five years they did. Franca said, "Now I know why I brought so much food and drink for a picnic for only the two of us! I must have sensed that I would meet you and your sons here." So the five of us had a fine picnic. Then she invited us to have supper at her house in Antignano. It was an older farmhouse – an old sharecropper's house, actually – that her family, which lived in Milano, and Gioia's family, which lived in Genoa, had bought together to use as a summer home.

In 1975, still further in the future, Dorothy and I and our two daughters, Rhea and Franca (I did not dare to suggest Gioia, but her sister's name was acceptable) stayed for a few days with Gioia and her family in Genoa. We also went to another country home they have in Sasello, in the hills northwest of Genoa, and then went to meet them in the country home in Antignano. It was a beautiful visit. Dorothy and Gioia got along very well. Whenever Dorothy's Italian was not adequate, they used German. For my part I was surprised at how similar they were, not only in character but even in looks and manners. We have always been in touch, and in the spring of 1997, Gioia's granddaughter, Barbara Levi, took time off from her postgraduate studies at Vassar to come and visit us for a week. We went skiing together and made some excursions in the Okanagan Valley.

10. *The Man from New York*

My time in Livorno was interspersed with a variety of experiences. For example, while I was still a Prisoner of War, the commanding officer of our office, Captain di Stefano, gave me one week's leave to go to Rome and visit with the Redivo family and with another family, that of Mr. Martino Bran, who was also originally from Roveredo. I had to hitchhike on an American military vehicle from Livorno to Rome, which was not too difficult, since I spoke English. Because times were very tough in Rome, especially regarding food, I could not impose myself for meals on the families I visited. All over Rome, though, there were specified restaurants designated as PX places, where American military personnel could eat while on leave or on duty in Rome. All they had to do was to enter their name, rank, serial number, and their service unit into a ledger at the entrance of the establishment. After that, they were given a chit for a meal. As soon as I took off the little metal POW insignia of the Italian Boot from my shirtsleeve, I looked like the other GI's. The rest was easy: I entered my name, rank, serial number (I had one as a POW – 81-I-32894, which I adjusted and made similar to those already in the ledger), and the name and the number of the American unit to which I was attached, and voila, I had my daily meals for the week I was in Rome. Of course this was not legal and I had to make sure that I was not caught – I was still a Prisoner of War and not entitled to make use of those facilities. To keep things straight, whenever I got into conversation with another American soldier who was eating there, my first question always was, "Where are you from and where all have you been in the States?" When he said, "From Boston," then I was from Seattle or Portland, Oregon. If he said, "San Francisco," then I was from New York, or from some other Eastern city. It worked!

I took another leave, still as a POW, in August 1945. That time I had received a postcard from a girl in Piombino – the embarkation point for the island of Elba. This girl's sister, Angela, had fallen in love with a German soldier, and when the Germans were driven back to the North, and later all the way into Germany, she went with him. Somehow during all these upheavals, however, they lost each other, and she ended up completely stranded in Germany. Some fate brought her to Dalheim, the village where my parents lived, and there she met my father, with whom she could speak Italian. Seeing the helplessness of the girl, my parents gave her shelter for the rest of the war. It was through Angela that her sister in Piombino got my POW address; she wrote to me and invited me to visit her and her aunt and uncle, which I did. While I was in Piombino, the first atom bomb was dropped on Hiroshima. I shall never forget the headline in the Italian newspaper. It was in big block letters across the front page: F E R M I. The reference was to the Italian scientist Enrico Fermi, who was living in exile in the United States – he had left Italy because of the fascist regime, and had an important role in developing the Atomic Bomb.

During my time in Livorno I also had what was for me an unusual "spiritual" experience. I made the acquaintance of two American soldiers. They were not from the office where I worked, but I met them somehow – somewhere I can no longer remember. I thought it would be helpful to have some American friends. We met a few times and everything appeared to be quite normal – until one Sunday evening when they invited me to come with them to their church service. Curious as I always was, I went along. Their church was a medium-sized hall with benches. A preacher was conducting the service. The congregation consisted entirely of American GI's. At the end of the service I heard the preacher praying to God that one of those present in the congregation should come forward to be "saved." He kept repeating that sentence. In time, it became hypnotic. Suddenly I realized that all eyes were on me and that I was the one to be saved. Since the chanting looked like it was going to be unending, I gathered my courage together and walked up the aisle towards the preacher. As soon as I did that the whole congregation started shouting, "Hallelujah! Praise to God!" and "Amen, Amen!" and so forth. I had to kneel down, where I was blessed. Then the service was finished.

When I walked out with my "friends," everybody congratulated me, and I received a small military edition of the New Testament. I don't even know what denomination this was, but it appeared to me to be an extreme sect. I was not willing to be part of it and therefore never saw my "friends" again.

Another memory of that time is of my almost daily trips to the beach to swim. There I became acquainted with some Italian officers who were not POW's, but were with the new Italian Army, established by the new Government of Marshal Badoglio under the King, and which was now an Allied army. It was a funny situation: I, the Italian POW of the Americans, and they, the officers of the Italian Army, which now was actually part of that army which had me in custody!

In July or the beginning of August I was released from the custody of the U.S. Army back to the regular Italian Army. I was still kept in Livorno, however, although now under Italian command. For work, I was put into an office to translate innumerable documents from English into Italian, mostly court-martial cases of Italian POW's. This was the most boring job I had ever had to do and in my opinion completely unnecessary. Fortunately, after a month I was sent to Orvieto, just north of Rome, for my honourable discharge. There I had to wait an extra month before I received my discharge papers, because my civilian residence was in Germany and at the end of the war the Allies had closed all German borders. Finally, I successfully convinced the officials issuing the discharge papers that I could go to my relatives, the Redivos in Roveredo in Piano. My honourable discharge paper is dated September 30, 1945.

No public transportation was functioning normally at that time, so I hitchhiked to Roveredo in northern Italy, at that time in the province of Udine. Because I was still wearing the American soldier's khaki uniform, but without the "Italian boot" insignia (this time legitimately!), I got rides easily. In one instance, a captain and his driver picked me up outside Firenze and took me as far as Bologna. At the halfway point we stopped at an American PX restaurant, where the captain invited me to eat supper with him. In those days, that was a real treat. Up to that point I was pretending that I was an American GI on a mission to some fictitious town in the North, but before I accepted his invitation for supper I confessed that I was Italian, that I had just been released from the Italian Army and was on my way home, and apologized. He accepted my apologies and invited me anyway. Afterwards, we continued on to Bologna, where I went to the railway station to sleep and to catch a train to

Pordenone, which is only seven kilometres from Roveredo. I arrived in Roveredo the next day in the evening. My aunts and their two sons, who were a little younger than I was, welcomed me, certainly, but when I saw how little they had to live on, and especially how sparse their food rations were, I could not in good conscience impose on them. After a visit of a couple of weeks I said good-bye and tried to travel to Germany and home to my parents.

When I arrived in the border city of Bolzano, again by hitchhiking and unpredictable train connections, I went to a British transition camp, where a British Officer was in charge of all border crossings. When I checked with him about my crossing into Germany and the possibility of obtaining some travel documents, he said, "I can let you pass only if you are a German citizen. You can now give me a statement in which you declare yourself German and you can go." Of course that is something I did not want to do, no matter how much I wanted to go home after an absence of over three years. So I stayed in Italy. Because I could not go back to my relatives in Roveredo, I decided to go to Rome, where I could see the Dionisio Redivo family and find out how I could manage to live there until things began to return to normal again. As *Reduce di Guerra*, a war veteran, I knew I could obtain some assistance.

Once in Rome, I discovered a place where I could pick up some civilian clothes (used clothing from American charity organizations), and found a place to stay in an Italian refugee camp. This camp was actually in the huge halls of Cinecittà, the famous Italian film studios on the outskirts of Rome. There I met other people who were in similar situations. Many were Italian families who had fled from Tunisia. All there was for each of us to sleep on was a *pagliariccio*, a sack filled with straw, and one blanket. We were given a daily ration of one round piece of good bread and about a pint of warm milk in the morning, made from powder. If we were still hungry we had to find our own ways to still our hunger. This I did by going from time to time to visit the Redivo and the Bran families, who were generous and encouraged me to come any time.

As soon as I had settled in at the refugee camp, I started looking for a job. There were always job offers posted by the American administration near the main train station; some of them required knowledge of English. One day, the motor pool of the Ciampino airport, at that time a military airport, had an opening for a typist who knew English. I went to apply for this job. When I arrived, there was a long line of applicants. I took my place in line. One at a time, applicants were called into the office to be interviewed. Getting closer to the spot where the people were interviewed, I noticed that there was a sergeant in charge and that the interview consisted of a typing test on an Underwood typewriter with an American keyboard. The sergeant asked the applicant to sit down and type something. Most of them asked, "What shall I type?"

"Just anything," was the sergeant's reply. Then the person would hesitantly try to think of something, start typing, not very fast, really, partly because they were thinking, but also because they were not used to the Underwood typewriter keyboard, which was different from that of the Italian Olivetti typewriter. After a minute or so of this, the sergeant would call out, "Next!" In this way the line moved forward very quickly.

When my turn came and the sergeant gave me the same order, I did not ask any questions, but sat down and typed a practice phrase, which I had practiced on an Underwood typewriter during my two years in an American Army office. The phrase filled exactly one line and read: "Now is the time for all good men to come to the aid of their country." At the end of the line, I flipped the carrier to the starting point again. I repeated this several times without looking at the typewriter but rather at the sergeant, who noticed my speed and that I was looking at him. He did not look at what I typed, but I was hired on the spot and the others were dismissed. My job was an easy one. Not much typing was needed to keep track of the vehicles that were assigned daily to various military personnel for various assignments. The pay was such that I could save some money, and I saved more by eating at the American mess at the airport. I was also able to buy some American cigarettes, which were a highly rated currency in those days. There were supposedly cases of American GI's buying entire houses with a few cartons of cigarettes or a few pairs of nylons.

From that time, I remember instances when jeeps had their tires stolen when left overnight on the streets of Rome. The jeeps were left in the evening in good shape, and the next morning they were sitting on four blocks, without wheels. At other times, when a Liberty Ship of supplies was unloaded in Naples onto trucks with Italian drivers to take them to the supply depots for storage, they never arrived. The empty trucks were found later in some remote region of the country.

The first week I was in Rome, I went to the Italian Ministry of Foreign Affairs and applied for my re-instatement as an employee of that Ministry. With this, I set the process in motion for my re-hiring. It took about three months. In the beginning of January 1945, I received notice that I was reinstated and that I could start working at the Ministry as soon as the re-instatement degree was signed. This took another month, after which I quit my job at the airport with the Americans and started working at the *Ministero degli Affari Esteri* (the Ministry of Foreign Affairs), which at that time was located in the famous Palazzo Chigi, at number 1 on the Corso Umberto, which is now just called Via del Corso. Up until then I lived at Cinecittà in the refugee camp, but now I could afford to rent a room in the city near the Ministry. My monthly pay at the Ministry was 8000 Lire a month, while the rent of my room was 3000 Lire a month. To put these prices into the proper perspective for those times, a meal cost about 200 Lire.

As soon as I started working at the Ministry, I applied for a transfer to a consulate, legation or embassy in a German or English-speaking country. While my request was under consideration, I was made responsible for the supplies in the staff bar, for the employees' coffee breaks and snacks. I had to seek out the black markets in Rome to find sugar, coffee, liqueurs, teas and whatever else was needed. Sometimes this was a risky operation. My boss, a retired colonel with only one eye, knew this, but asked me to do the best I could, and promised that I would be rescued if I was arrested for my illegal black market activities. As it turned out, I managed all right. After my time in the refugee camp, those were good times for me as a civilian, in a regular apartment, in that big, beautiful city of Rome. Due to my earlier stay in Rome as a soldier in the interpreter company (from September 1942 to March 1943), I was quite familiar with the city. What's more, I re-established the earlier contact I had with the Redivo family, which gave me a social life.

Two details stick out in my mind. The Redivo sons, Duilio, Arturo, and Romeo, had their friends and sisters, and the friends had sisters, and thus I was accepted in a very happy circle. On the weekends they organized dances in private homes, and so I got to know Marcella, the sister of one of Duilio's friends. To have a date with her and to see her alone was impossible, though. We did meet once on a Monday morning in front of the Cathedral San Giovanni in Leterano. She had skipped school and we walked for a couple of hours together, but that was all, and it was the only time we met alone.

Another friendship that developed out of my being accepted in that circle of friends was with Antonietta Minafra, a beautiful dark-haired and dark-eyed girl. To see her alone was only possible if I went to the 11:00 o'clock Sunday Mass in her church, which she attended with her mother. At 12:00 o'clock, she would give her mother some excuse about an errand, or meeting a friend, but promised to be home for lunch in half an hour. That was the only way we could see each other, on a Sunday – for half an hour. Under the circumstances that prevailed at that time there just wasn't much chance to get more involved with a girl, but I was happy to have these friendships, considering that I was alone in this big city and had no idea when and if ever I would be able to go home to Germany.

Only once did I become really homesick. It was on Christmas Day, 1945. I was still living in the refugee camp. The night before, I was with the Redivo family for supper, and then I went to midnight mass with them. The next day I could not impose again on their kind hospitality, so I rode the streetcar from my refugee camp into the city, to walk through the city to distract myself from the thought that it was Christmas. In my whole life up until that time I had never felt so lonely as during those few hours I meandered through the mostly empty streets, past all those old historical monuments, palaces, churches and familiar fountains. When I returned to the refugee camp, it too was almost empty, and I wondered if there ever would be better days ahead. I continued patiently waiting for my job at the Ministry of Foreign Affairs, which occurred shortly after Christmas.

My meagre salary of 8000 Lire a month at the Ministry was not enough, however, to support myself and live a normal life. As I struggled along, though, my request for a transfer was granted, and on July 5, 1946 I left Rome by train for my new post at the Italian Legation in Bern, Switzerland. I was absolutely delighted to be going to a country that had escaped the war and all its devastations. Crossing the border at Domodossola into Switzerland was like leaving the ordinary world behind and arriving in *Schlaraffenland*, a land where milk and honey flows. Although my salary there was minimal, only 295 Swiss Franks a month, I had a room at the Legation at no cost. And of course the mere fact of living in Switzerland from July 5, 1945 on, so shortly after the devastating war all across Europe, was a great privilege and a blessing that more than compensated for the low salary.

11. You Smell So Funny

My time in Switzerland, from July 1946 to April 1949, was very reward-ing in many ways. It was a new beginning in my life that had been controlled by war for four years. I didn't consider those war years wasted years, how-ever, since I had learned a lot and had gained much life experience.

In Switzerland, my ambition was to advance in the hierarchy of the Ital-ian Foreign Ministry. Because of my knowledge of Italian and English, in ad-dition to my mother tongue, I was holding down a secure job as receptionist, but I wanted to go back to school to complete my education and obtain my Abitur (high school diploma – a European university entry requirement). I never could manage to budget the time to realize this dream. One reason was that I met "that" Swiss girl, who came regularly to the Italian Consulate, ap-plying for visas for the "Swiss Relief" organization for which she worked. My free time wasn't enough to both court this girl and go to school.

In Bern, my German was not always an advantage. I was very surprised when I arrived from Italy at the Bern train station. When I stepped out on the street to catch a streetcar, the people whom I asked in perfect High German for directions treated me very rudely. When I asked one newspaper vendor, who was crying out, *"Der Bund! Der Bund!"* (a Bernese newspaper), he mut-tered under his breath, *"Sau Schwob"* ("Schwabian – or German – Pig!"), and did not give me directions. I had the same experience when I went into stores or restaurants. I asked questions or ordered food in a polite way in perfect High German, but in most cases I was either ignored or treated very indiffer-ently. This difficulty did not last long: I soon figured out that because of the war the Swiss hated anything that came from Germany or seemed German. They hated the language most of all, because all Swiss Germans speak Schwitzerdütch, which is and sounds very different from High German, al-though their newspapers are printed in perfect high German: a sure recipe for conflict. Even though I had been happy to come to a country where I could speak German again, I realized very soon that in Bern, an almost bilingual city, I would be better off if I learned to speak French. After that, I tried to get around in that language.

Another factor in my decision was that at that time French was still the diplomatic language of the world. In most cases, people who came to the reception wicket at the Italian Legation stated their business in French. So did "that" girl, and the first conversations I had with her were in French, until I discovered that she actually spoke German and, what's more, not only *Schwitzerdütch* but high German as well, or what the Swiss call *Schriftdeutsch* – written German. Through two years of persistent courting, the girl, Dorothy Vögeli, became my wife and over time the mother of our four children.

As I mentioned, we met through the receptionist wicket at the Italian Legation, speaking French to each other (mine poor and hers perfect) until, after a few encounters, we realized that we both spoke better German. After some time, Dorothy noticed that I was wearing riding boots, a leftover from my Young Fascist uniform. She asked me if I ever went horseback riding. Not suspecting anything, but just thinking that there was an interest in me, I answered in a very sure and matter-of-fact manner, "Oh yes, I ride," which was a young man's boast, and a lie, too. At that, with some enthusiasm, Dorothy invited me to come riding with her and her friends, and mentioned that she loved horses. Despite being slightly shocked, I accepted her invitation. This was a first date with her, and on top of that, one which she had initiated. I could not refuse, and we arranged to go riding.

When the time came, we went to the stable that rented out the horses. I was a little apprehensive as to how things would unfold, because, except when I had been a little five- or six-year-old boy on a farm workhorse in the country, I had never sat on a horse before. I went to the stable master, Monsieur Lèchot, a French-Swiss, and asked him to please give me a fairly tame horse, as this was my first time riding. Smart as he was, he sensed immediately that I had come there with Dorothy to impress her, and, since he had a bit of a crush on her himself, he gave me a rather stubborn horse, with which I had great difficulties. Of course Dorothy noticed right away that I was no rider, ignored me completely, and went along with the others, who all were experienced riders, while I struggled with my stubborn horse. I learned my lesson then and there, to stop pretending and exaggerating.

After that experience, I went on my own without Dorothy's knowledge to another stable and rented a horse, to practice handling these animals. I even went so far as to take some riding lessons. Unfortunately, that was not a success. The instructor was a former Swiss cavalry officer; when he noticed that I could not speak Swiss German, he ridiculed me in front of others, scolded me, and in general treated me very abusively. After three or four lessons I gave up, but it did give me a little more practice, and Dorothy and I did go out riding a few times in the beautiful and forested surroundings and parks of the city of Bern. Through these outings we got to know each other a little better, and it became time to drop the formalities of "Mr. Redivo" and "Miss Vögeli" and to get on a more informal first name basis. In German, this change includes a whole change in the language, because at the same time one must change from the formal *Sie*, the formal form of "you," to the more familiar du, and must change every verb form with it. This changeover was one of our funny moments, because I asked, "May I address you with 'du' and your first name?" When she did not reply but looked at me hesitantly, I caught myself. I realized that because of the way I had said it she thought I meant that I should call her by her first name, yet expected her to still call me "Mr. Redivo," so I added right away, "Of course, this is meant reciprocally." Then she agreed.

Another awkward moment came with our first kiss. At the time I was smoking cigarettes, cigars and occasionally a pipe. When for the first time she finally consented to let me come close enough to give her a kiss, she pulled her head back and said, "You smell so funny," and so this first kiss was not really a proper kiss! After this incident it was clear to me that if I wanted to kiss this girl I would have to quit smoking. This I did on the spot. When I came back to the office I gave away the rest of an open package of cigarettes, a couple of cigars, and sold my pipe for twenty Swiss Franks. I figured the choice was either kissing or smoking. For me there was no choice. (We still kiss.)

The first time I invited Dorothy to dine out with me I noticed that she did not order any meat, while I ordered a steak. When I finally asked her why she did not eat any meat, she told me that during the war she had pet rabbits in the garden and one day one of her pet rabbits was on the table to be eaten. She did not eat that night. Besides the emotional upset, her main reason was that all meat comes from an animal that once was alive, like her rabbit, and had to be killed to provide the meat. I had never thought about that, but the story touched me so much that I stopped eating meat, too. I have never missed it.

Because Dorothy came regularly to the Italian Legation, we saw each other often. We went for lunch together (which she often supplied) in the Dalhölzli Park on the Aare River, and dated regularly. One time, I was so bold as to sing under her second-storey window. I don't know what her landlady thought, but knowing that I was Italian, perhaps she was not too surprised.

Another time we exchanged accountings of our finances. To my surprise, I discovered that she had saved 5,000 Sfr. from her salary of about 450 Sfr. a month, whereas I could save nothing from my 295 Sfr. salary. Of course my smaller salary made saving more difficult, but still her savings account was intimidating. However, shortly afterwards I had a windfall in back pay. When I started my job, my salary was still geared to the prewar wages and exchange rates of the Swiss and Italian currencies. As time passed, however, this discrepancy had been corrected and my monthly salary more than doubled to about 650 Sfr., and, what's more, the increase was retroactive to the date when I started in Bern. I now too had about 5,000 Sfr. in the bank and felt much better about it. Having some money in the bank, and with Dorothy's encouragement, I also learned to save money and not to spend it on every whim.

My position at the Italian Legation was not very satisfying. The chances to advance in the hierarchy were slim, and the legation was filled with jealousy, intrigue and humiliation. I had to cater to every whim of the upper functionaries. The secretaries of the Legation were under the Minister, the Charge d'Affaire. On duty as receptionist and *usciere*, I had to answer calls and go to the offices from which the calls originated. On one occasion, the buzzer rang from the office of the First Secretary, which in rank is second-in-command after the Minister. The First Secretary's name was Count Pletti. When I entered the room and asked what he required, he asked me to pick up one page that had dropped on the floor from a newspaper he was reading. All he had to do was bend over and reach for it himself. To my mind, it was a humiliating

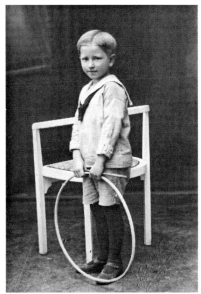

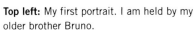

Top left: My first portrait. I am held by my older brother Bruno.
Top right: A professional portrait of me taken on my sixth birthday.
Above left: The house in Dalheim which my father built for us in 1925.
Right: This photograph reflects the rough times we experienced in Germany after the crash of the Stock Exchange in New York.

Top: A group photo of grades 5, 6, 7 and 8, taken in 1932. I am to the right of the teacher, in a dark jacket with a white collar.

Above left: My mother Else Redivo, nee Pörtner.

Above middle: My father Domenico Pasquale Redivo.

Above right: My brother Bruno Giovanni Redivo.

Right: At the completion of my apprenticeship I received this officially-stamped booklet with my final marks.

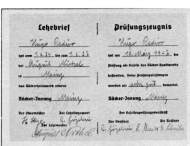

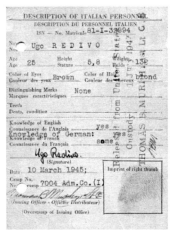

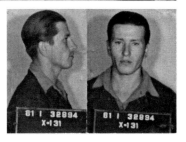

Top: Me (centre) in my Italian Artillerist's uniform on the streets in Rome (1942).
Above left: Still in Frankfurt, I am with the Italian Consul's "Lancia," in which I accompanied the chauffeur to pick up Princess Mafalda in Bad Orb.
Above: My POW ID card, which I received after the Italian armistice in 1943.
Left: My ID photos taken by the American Army when I became a POW.

HEADQUARTERS
2694TH TECHNICAL SUPERVISION REGIMENT (OVHD)
APO 782   U. S. ARMY

23 June 1945

MEMORANDUM:

TO   : Major Benedict S. Alper,
            WMD & IPOW Sub-Comm.,
            Allied Commission,
            APO 394, U. S. Army.

    1. Attached hereto for your information is a copy of a
letter written by Pvt. Ugo Redivo, 81-I-32894, to the Italian
Ministry of War requesting to be released from any future
service in the Italian Army.

    2. It is believed that the Italian Army has little claim
to hold this man as he was born and raised in Germany. He
became an Italian citizen merely because his birth was registered with an Italian Consulate in Germany as his father was
of Italian birth and his mother a German.

    3. Pvt. Redivo has been completely loyal to the U. S.
Army since August of 1943. It is considered that he has been
thoroughly converted to the democratic way of life and we
would like to assist him in his desire to return to Germany.
He will always be a friend of the U. S. and we feel that we
will need to have friends in Germany.

    4. It would be appreciated if you would advise us if it
would be possible to have Redivo classified as a "displaced
person" and returned to Frankfurt am Main, Germany, subsequent
to his eventual release from the Italian Army.

                              J. DE STEFANO,
                              Capt., Inf.

*Certified true copy of letter
received in this Hq. AWHamilton
                    Maj.*

*Hq. 2694
AE. 15/04/45*

Above: A letter from Capt. De Stefano. In paragraph three he vouches that I have been loyal to the U.S. Army and appear to have been thoroughly converted to the democratic way of life.
Left: With two other Italian POW's and a smiling American corporal. I am on the right.

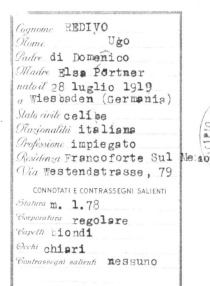

Top: My first post-war civilian ID card, issued by the community of Roveredo, my father's home town.
Left: I am in GI uniform in Rome (1945), on leave from my POW office duties in Livorno.
Above: I received this Ministry ID card after I was re-hired by the Italian Ministry of Foreign Affairs.

Top: Marina Grande, the port of Capri, and the grandiose scenery from the balcony of our hotel in Annacapri.
Above left: Dorothy at the entrance of the San Michele Museum, the former home of Swedish physician and naturalist Axel Munthe.
Left: Dorothy in a holiday mood in Portovenere, near La Spezia.
Above: Dorothy and I in Neuchâtel, on one of our first dates.

Top: Our wedding on October 16, 1948, in the Protestant church in Hombrechtikon.

Above left: Our last visit with my parents in Dalheim, before we left for Canada.
Above right: With Dorothy's parents before our departure.

Top: The pages in my Italian passport containing my Canadian Immigration Visa and all my necessary exit and entry stamps.

Above left: With our carry-on luggage on board the CPR ship "Empress of France" in the port of Liverpool.
Above right: Dorothy on board with our luggage.

Top: Our first brief exploration of Canada during a tour of Quebec City.
Above: Our arrival in Artland. There was not another soul at the station.
Right above: With Ruth and Otto Wüthrich and our steward, just before disembarkation in Montreal.
Right below: Dorothy and Uncle Henry in the port of Vancouver before leaving for Surge Narrows.

Top left: Dorothy proudly in front of her work – the wash line.
Top right: A snapshot of me roofing Henry's woodshed.
Bottom: Our first dwelling in the Okanagan – the Pearson's boathouse on Okanagan Lake.

Top: The happy couple ready for adventure in their new land.
Middle right: Dorothy in front of the Grundigs' cabin, where we lived for three winters.
Bottom right: Here I am getting our water from a spring, about fifty yards from the cabin.

Top left: Out photographing with my first Rolleicord, purchased for $180, when I earned 65 cents an hour.

Top right: Learning how to prune fruit trees on Mr. Karrer's orchard.

Above left: A snapshot of me, our tent in Fort St. John, and the carpenter's tool box I made.

Above right: Dorothy looking out of the tent under five inches of snow on August 15, 1950.

Top left: Even earning only 50 cents an hour while picking fruit, Dorothy was happy.
Top right: In their modern living room, Tilly Grundig serves Alfred, Dorothy and our friend Betty Leinor.
Above left: A glimpse of German-Canadian life on Naramata Road – having tea in the Wendenburg's garden.
Above right: Alfred Gruhl, orchardist and hobby painter – our friend since 1950.
Right: Our two best friends, Fritz Pruesse and Alfred Grundig, second and third from left.

Greetings **CAMEO STUDIOS**

Xma, 1955

Top left: The Pruesses' house above Skaha Lake, where we moved after Marcus was born in 1952 and which we left after Selwyn was born in 1954 to make room for the Leipes.

Top right: Here I am, busy plastering the Pruesse's house in lieu of rent.

Middle left: While out of work I carried on with freelance photography.

Bottom left: Our store, after I bought out Bob Morrison and the name changed to "Redivo Camera Centre and Studio."

Above: Our first Christmas ad, showing Harry Killick, me (standing), and Bob Morrison (with his Press camera).

Top: The victorious Vees are welcomed at the Penticton airport.
Left: With my 16mm Bolex Movie Camera that I used for twelve years as CBC news reporter.
Above: My family in Germany, during our visit in 1959, including one-year-old Rhea.

Top: Dorothy's sister's family, before our return to Canada.
Bottom: "Casa Miralago," our dream house on Skaha Lake. We moved in in May 1961, a month before our fourth child, Franca, was born. We still live in this house in 2006.

and an uncalled-for request. He was an Italian count, but in my view not an aristocrat at all. It was probably then and there that I decided that this job, in which I had to suffer such humiliations, was not for me. Another humiliation was that the Second Secretary used to send me on unnecessary errands; he was annoyed because I could receive English-speaking diplomats in fluent English, whereas his proficiency in that language was halting.

Since I had relatives in Argentina, I contemplated immigrating to that country if my attempts to go to the United States failed. As I mentioned earlier, T-Sergeant Victor Barret, who I befriended in the POW Camp in Africa, sponsored me, as did a major in the U.S. Army who I met in Livorno. However, as long as these men were in the Occupation Army in Europe they would not be in the States to look after me, as was required by an affidavit of sponsorship. In the meantime, Dorothy was in correspondence with her Uncle Henry Hess in Canada, and formulated the idea of possibly immigrating there. Her job at the relief agency had been terminated, and she was looking for other opportunities. At that time, she was living with her family in Hombrechtikon, near Zurich. Even though Dorothy and I were very close by that time, I would have never dared to ask her to marry me. The main reason was that I could not assume the responsibility of taking away her Swiss citizenship. In those days a Swiss woman would lose her status as a Swiss and assume the nationality of the husband she married. The Swiss passport was the most precious document one could possess in postwar Europe and she would have become Italian once she married me (which she later did).

Another option became open to me through a Mrs. Koch, a Quaker from Philadelphia, whom Dorothy had met and who said she could provide another sponsor for me, a very good one. Shortly after that I received mail from Mr. Martin F. Emory of Westport, Connecticut, in which he confirmed that he was in the process of preparing the papers for the necessary affidavit. This was in September 1948. I had one more letter from him confirming the progress, then I heard no more, despite writing to him several times to ask at what point things stood. By this time, however, Dorothy had decided to immigrate to Canada and had started to communicate with her uncle about her intention. It was then that I decided that I wanted to go with her. Dorothy communicated the news to her uncle. Knowing now that we would both soon leave Europe to start a new life in Canada, we decided to become engaged. We made this decision in Olten, after hiking up a mountain and declaring our love for each other – in Olten because I came from Bern and Dorothy from Hombrechtikon: Olten was central. The date was September 5, 1948. Her uncle had only to write a letter to the Canadian Minister of Immigration in Ottawa and declare that he had employment for us for one year on his farm, which he still owned in Marsden, Saskatchewan. He did not mention that he had leased the farm to a neighbour. At that time, in 1948, the Canadian immigration laws stated that one could immigrate into Canada only as a miner, logger or farmer. We went as farmers. At this moment the prospects to acquire our permanent residence visas for Canada looked pretty sure.

As Canada had no diplomatic representation yet in Switzerland to interview prospective immigrants and issue visas, a C.P.R. agent visited the Swiss Travel Agency Kehrli und Öhler twice a year to interview people for the Canadian Government. This gentleman was a Mr. Watson, who not only interviewed us but with whom we also had to book our passage. During the interview we inquired about the cost of the passage, to which he replied that the least expensive single cabin would be Cdn. $143, but if we were married we could be both in the same cabin and save Cdn. $143. Dorothy and I looked at each other (we had never discussed a marriage date) and decided then and there to get married before leaving for Canada. So, on October 16, 1948 we were married in Hombrechtikon.

Meanwhile, the Italian Legation in Bern wanted to lay off one of my colleagues with less seniority, because his department of the Consulate General, which was in the same building as mine, was over-staffed. When I heard that, and since I was now sure of obtaining my visa for Canada, I offered to quit my job on the same day this colleague would be laid off, if my leaving would allow him to keep his job. The Minister, Professor Egidio Reale, said yes, and found this a noble gesture on my part. He even gave me a letter of commendation. Thus, on September 30, 1948 I left the employment of the Italian Ministry of Foreign Affairs to embark on an unknown and unpredictable adventure. All the others at the legation thought I was crazy to leave such a secure and well-paid job, with pensions, holidays and lots of extraterritorial privileges. For one thing, we paid no taxes, neither in Switzerland nor in Italy. Dorothy, however, would not have liked to be the wife of a little employee who had to dance to the whim of everybody above him and live with the jealousies and intrigues of the system.

When, after ten years in Canada, I came back to visit all those who thought I was crazy to give up my secure job, they were rather envious, because I came back with a wife and three children, had a well-established photography business in Canada, and could afford to make the trip to Europe (which in those days was extremely expensive), while they were still doing the same old things: issuing passports and visas, stamping passports with renewals, and so forth.

12. The Blue Grotto

*I*n Switzerland I was living not all that far from Dalheim and my parents. To get there, however, was rather complicated. After the war the Allies had sealed off Germany and had divided it into four different occupation zones: American, English, French and Russian. My parents lived in the French Zone. To travel there I needed a French visa. To get one, I had to apply to the Bern office of the French Occupation Force. Finally, with the help of one of the secretaries of the legation, I was able to obtain a visa – valid from October 18 to November 5, 1946 – so I could take the train across the border to visit my parents and my brother and his family. I hadn't seen them for over four years. Fortunately, since they were living in a small village they had not suffered much during the war: the Americans had just plowed through without a fight, on their rush to the Rhine.

My parents, I discovered, were not alone in their house; they were sharing it with people who had been bombed out in Mainz. When I visited Mainz, I could not believe the destruction from the bombing and the general ravage of the war. It was difficult to recognize the layout of the streets with which I once was so familiar – whole blocks were nothing but rubble. In some parts of the city, I was completely disoriented. Some people were living in basements or even in holes in the ground. It was unbelievable, yet some structures were still standing and intact: the famous Mainzer Dom (the cathedral), for instance, was somewhat damaged but not destroyed.

After this brief visit to Germany, I felt fortunate to be able to return to Switzerland. From there I was able to send home some of the necessities they were very short of in Germany. Food they had, because, even though food was still rationed in Germany, they lived in the country, but there were many other things that they could not buy. Flints were particularly sought after items; they served as currency. Coffee, tea and sugar were also rare and much in demand, and were also used for bartering.

In June 1947, Dorothy and I made a plan to take a holiday in Italy. The trip lasted from June 3 to June 18. Before she agreed to come with me, Dorothy laid down some strict conditions: we each would have to pay our own way, we would have different bedrooms, and I would not attempt to become intimate with her – in other words, I would not try to seduce her. I had no choice but to agree!

My plan was to first visit Gioia and family in Livorno, then to visit the Redivo family in Rome, then to spend the rest of the holidays, another eight days, in Naples and on the Isle of Capri. We arrived in Livorno at a truly ungodly hour, and spent the rest of that night on a park bench near the railroad station. Then we looked for a hotel. When we finally found one with a vacancy, only one room – with a double bed – was available. The receptionist, who most likely was also the owner, asked for our passports; when he saw one Italian and one Swiss passport he realized that we were not married and was reluctant to give us the room. In the end, though, he did. Dorothy was uncomfortable with the arrangement, but saw that there was no other choice. I assured her that I would keep my promise, even if we slept in the same bed, which we did. I kept this promise during the entire two weeks of our holiday, because from then on we always booked into one room. Sometimes we had twin beds, whenever they were available.

It was on this trip that we visited the Santarini family, but did not meet Gioia. This also was the time when Dorothy, who was totally exhausted, slept on Gioia's bed. From Livorno we proceeded to Rome. We traveled by night and were in a compartment with six other people, who were all more or less sleeping. It was a moonlit night. Seeing that everyone appeared to be sleeping, we went out into the corridor to admire the moonlit landscape. Unfortunately, Dorothy left her purse on the seat. She had two 100 Sfr. notes in her wallet. The next time she used it, it held only one 100 Sfr. note. To this day, she is convinced that whoever stole the one note was considerate enough to leave her the other one so that she would not be left with nothing.

We arrived in Rome, checked into a hotel near the Piazza di Spagna, and promptly took a walk, via the Spanish Steps, towards the Villa Borghese Park. It was there that by sheer coincidence we ran into Prince Pignatelli who was in the Prisoner of War camp with me in Africa. We both were surprised to meet so unexpectedly in this big city, with its two million inhabitants. We reminisced about our time together in North Africa and lamented the fact that we both would have been in the officers' camp, and would have received officers' pay, if we had been captured after we had received our commissions. It was always a pleasure to talk with the Roman prince, who had had to fit in with us ordinary soldiers. He had adapted well and we respected him because of it.

While in Rome, we also met briefly with Arturo and Duilio Redivo. I brought Arturo a Swiss watch he had wished for before I had left Rome for Switzerland. We did not see the rest of the family, because we were short of time and had to leave for Naples the same day. The brothers were hospitable and showed us a little of Rome, but because of the time restraint we saw only a few sites. We shared an espresso and exchanged some recent news. We sensed strongly that they were rather envious of us for living in a country like Switzerland, without war ruins, and where daily life was stable. When we said good-bye, I promised to visit again, sometime. (This I did, with our two sons, twenty-three years later.)

In Naples we checked into a hotel, *La Patria*, and then went on to visit Pompeii and Herculaneum. A guide showed us around and explained the history of these cities and how they were covered with lava and ashes in 70 A.D. While we toured this impressive archaeological site a funny thing happened to Dorothy: when she bent down somewhere to view some plants, a twig of myrtle stuck to her hair. Myrtle is a southern European shrub, with evergreen leaves, fragrant white flowers and aromatic berries. It is used as an emblem of love and in ancient times was believed to be sacred to Venus, the goddess of love. When the guide saw the twig in Dorothy's hair, he said that was a sign that we would soon be married. Dorothy took the twig home and included it in a photo album of our trip, which she prepared and gave me for Christmas in 1947. It is over half a century ago now, but I still treasure that gift.

From Naples we took a boat to the Isle of Capri. We arrived at Marina Grande, the lower part of Capri, took the funicular, *il funicolare*, made famous from the song, "Funiculi, funicula," up to Capri proper, and booked into the hotel *Belvedere e Tre Re*. Except for one other visitor, we were the only guests in the entire hotel. It was wonderful: we had a room with a balcony, right on top of the island, with a view directly above the sea, overlooking Capri and the Gulf of Naples. The food and the service were excellent. The dining room was cozy, but not too elegant, with white tablecloths and fine cutlery, and was so situated that from our table we could look out across a balcony to the Mediterranean, the distant mainland, and Vesuvius. For meals, we enjoyed typical Italian pasta dishes, fresh vegetables, fresh seafood and a good glass of Italian wine. At times we were the only people dining, and with friendly Vincenzo serving – and as we were in love – we truly were in paradise. It was as if the world was there only for us. There was nothing to distract us from each other. It was an unforgettable experience.

After we had checked in at the hotel we explored our immediate surroundings, and it was then that Dorothy suddenly confessed that she had left her "things," which she would need at certain times during a month, with her other luggage in the hotel in Naples. Because she could not speak Italian well enough to deal with storekeepers, and could not really tell me about her situation, she did not know what to do. Since I had never before had to deal with such matters, I did not know much about them, either. I resolved to explain everything to Vincenzo, the waiter in the hotel. He was very understanding and without batting an eye provided Dorothy with the necessary items. Yes, she was a little embarrassed, but she was also very grateful that her problem was solved.

Due to Dorothy's condition, she did not go swimming in the sea. Instead, we hired a fisherman to take us in his rowboat into the "Blue Grotto," or the *Grotta azzurra*, as it is called in Italian. It is a cave in the rock wall of the island, accessible only through a small opening through which a small rowboat can enter during a calm sea. The deep blue of the water is amazing. To swim inside this cave is eerie. I swam there, while Dorothy sat on the rocks and watched, wishing that she could be swimming with me.

Capri was the home of the Roman Emperor Tiberius. The island is a rock, with steep limestone cliffs all around, and has always attracted the rich and famous, something Dorothy and I did not know when we chose to go there. In 1947, Italy was slowly recovering from the devastating war, and tourism was practically nonexistent. As we were about the only guests in our hotel, the people, servants, and shopkeepers of the island were all friendly and eager to please, which certainly helped the romantic atmosphere. We went on extensive walks up and down (literally) the roads, took horse-drawn coach rides, and indulged in the open views from the many different spots of that beautiful island. Of course, during these carefree days we got to know each other better and developed a closer relationship.

We visited the famous Museum of San Michele. It was built by Axel Munthe, a Swedish physician who studied in Sweden and France and became Physician to the Swedish Royal Family, especially to their Queen, Victoria. When Munthe was eighteen years old he visited the island and decided to build a house there, which he did. He called it San Michele. He was an author and a nature lover, and created sanctuaries for migratory birds, both on Capri and in Sweden. His book *The Story of San Michele* deals with his experiences as a physician and as a human being; it was translated into forty-seven languages. His humanity was perhaps one of the reasons we went to Capri, since we had heard about him in Switzerland. The other was that Dorothy was always interested and protective of birds. After all, her maiden name was "Vögeli" – little bird.

On our return trip, we left the train in La Spezia, and went down to the port. Around the port itself we saw several partly submerged warships, which had been bombed by the Allies. To see the bombed-out ships was a shock to the Swiss girl. Because she lived in neutral Switzerland, she had never been exposed directly to the devastation of war. It made Dorothy appreciate how lucky she was to be Swiss.

From La Spezia we took a boat to Portovenere, an old fishing village with a protective harbour. The town crawls up the rugged hills behind the harbour, and is crowned by a medieval castle and an old church, *San Pietro*. We stayed in another fine hotel, *Albergo Locanda S. Pietro*, and here, at last, we could swim together. We hired a fisherman to row us across a narrow strait to the island of Palmaria to swim. Again we had chosen an out-of-the-way spot to be alone. We hiked in the hills and up to the castle and explored Byron's Grotto, named after the English poet who had visited there in the previous century and who was inspired by its beautiful setting. In June 1947, there were no tourist crowds, and, just as it was in Capri, every moment was a unique and private experience.

13. *Merry Christmas!*

Here is what Dorothy wrote with the photographs from that trip to Italy in June of 1947:

Italy:

Two seats were reserved on the Italian Express from Bern, for June the 3rd, 1947, but, as is so often the case, they were occupied. The two travelers weren't sure what to do, and looked at each other questioningly, unsure whether it would be proper to take the two empty seats near the window instead.

As soon as the hands of the station clock struck the hour of departure, the wheels started moving and the train left the station. Is it true? Yes, we are leaving for Italy! Soon Bern is far behind us. Thunersee ... Kandersteg ... Wallis ... Simplon ... brilliant sunshine accompanies us. Already our compartment has an Italian air to it, and before we know it the customs officers are knocking. Anything to declare? "No." Passports ... "OK. Have a nice trip!"

I am a little girl peeking into a room full of grown-ups. You feel at home and want to show me your homeland. I am excited to think what you have in store for me!

Domodossola: the first deep breath of a foreign land ... Money exchange ... New tickets for the train. There is even enough time for a short walk outside the station, and for a first espresso. Before long, though, the trip continues, and the Alps slowly disappear behind us. Beautiful villas and heavenly gardens pass by. Workers with their black hair and sun-browned bodies – standing or lying near the stations – wave to us. All is new, yet familiar. Reality is not disappointing, even when compared to the images I have held for so long in my imagination. The same goes for the families in the railroad stations: torn clothes, a few bundles of baggage, and a baby with its milk bottle. And the faces behind the black railroad car windows, too – hadn't one seen them in the past, somewhere?

A quick peek out in front of the Milan train station, a refreshing frappe, and then on we go again! Happy to the tips of one's fingers and full of anticipation, one squishes past other passengers to get a little room to sit on the bench. The train hurtles across the fertile and magnificent Po River plain. One ought to have a few more eyes so one wouldn't have to let so much fly past without seeing it!

Soon the night descends and I try to find a spot to put my head down to sleep for a little while. But not for long! Soon the moon starts to enchant the lonely, rocky mountains and the valleys of the Apennines with its silvery light. While the monotone rhythm of the moving train goes on, I stare for hours into this silvery light, on and on, and already the first rays of the sun are touching the highest mountaintops and soon we will arrive in Rome. Tired and dirty, we leave the train. Rome! How often I have dreamed of this city!

But we are going to go on just the same – on to our destination, to Capri. After a day of meandering through the streets of Rome, the end of the day finds us sitting in the train again and traveling towards Naples. My eyes are tired from the many new impressions, but that evening they are granted their first glimpse of the sea.

But then, "Look out!" The busyness and confusion, which I already know well from reading newspapers and books, is all around us in the station at Naples. "No, I don't need anything!" Soon we stand in front of the hotel that was recommended to us, the La Patria, and are looking forward to what are by now really necessary hours of rest.

My first sea journey! Before long, Naples lies behind us, enveloped in haze, and we are traveling along the Gulf of Naples, passing Vesuvius. The volcano seems to be quiet, however, for not even a trace of smoke betrays its inner fires.

Sorrento. The houses seem to be built into the rocks. They seem to be glued to the narrow shore. In the port, we are offered beautiful souvenirs, but we can see our destination in the distance, the Isle of Capri, and before long our ship slides into its home port: "Marina Grande."

Here, too, we follow advice and recommendations, and we aren't disappointed. This postcard here shows the hotel, and these pictures tell the story of our experiences in Capri. Here's the great Terrace, with its view of the port and the open sea. May I introduce our best friends? Vincenzo and his dog Gypsy. It's the first evening, but you are already going out for a holiday swim in the sea, and now, together with Vincenzo, here we are visiting the festively decorated village of Capri. Only when it's very late do we let the melodies of the splashing waves lull us into sleep.

The Blue Grotto. Pietro rows us there, in a little rowboat that is like a nutshell. He takes time to entertain himself – and us, too. Here we are being regaled with mother-of-pearl ornaments and embroidered drapes as souvenirs of the "Blue Cave." For a moment, one just thinks these people are shrewd business people, but then, it has to be that way, doesn't it: it belongs to the fairy tale. Look, swimming in this blue, transparent water, you look like a merman!

It is hard to know if one is bewitched already, or if it's just that one will be soon. Can you not see it on these two children? *(Two pictures [not included].)*

In the afternoon, we travel to Anacapri in a horse-drawn coach. Every place, practically every stone, has its history. Everywhere lie mementos of Tiberius, whose story is so famous every little boy knows it. This is the portal of the San Michele Museum. *(Photo [not included].)* Everything seems so timeless, or seems to be living in the past. You feel that you have learned about so many legends here, about saints and bad men, that you must have been transported into a dreamland. Let's cast one last long glance over that island garden of paradise. *(Photo [not included].)*

On the other side of the island, where we have a view of the Faraglioni, the horse is trotting downhill. Beautiful villas, owned by people from all over the world, cover the hillside, surrounded by lovely gardens. Below them are the fishermen's houses of Marina Piccola. In Capri we can't resist the heavily stocked shops and their inviting brilliant colours. So many beautiful things are asking us to buy them! We accept their invitation, rather than taking the donkey ride we had planned.

Heavily laden, and accompanied by Vincenzo, we take the funicolare back from Marina Grande.

The last night – the last deferential serving by Vincenzo at the table – comes much too quickly. A tear tries to sneak into the eyes, but then, there is so much new awaiting us. Sad but happy, I admire the flowers which Vincenzo puts in my hands, and together we step on the little freighter that is going to take us back to the mainland. A last view of Capri. Arrivederci! The boat rides on big waves into the open sea, which gives a premonition what a real big ocean voyage would be like. But it is pleasant!

Soon the boat reaches the coast again, and cruises along the steep rock walls to Castellamare. From here, a horse-drawn coach takes us on a dizzying ride to Pompeii. We are in the past again, strolling through the dead city, viewing ancient skeletons and inhaling gases rising through a narrow passageway, directly from Hell. Even here, innumerable sagas and legends surround us. Regrettably, it has grown too late for us to be able to pay a visit to Vesuvius, so, in the evening, tired, we climb onto the train, which takes us back from Pompeii to Naples. The next day is a Sunday – it will be a day of rest for us, too.

After a Sunday stroll through the streets of the city, we find our steps drawn uphill so we can look at the city from above. There are innumerable, poor, broken-down and smelly dwellings, but the sun shines over the whole scene, and in the background is the sea. A streetcar takes us to the Posillipo, a short ride. Very far in the hazy distance we can make out the Isle of Capri. Here is the Isle of Nisida. *(Photo [not included].)* Here you can enjoy a wonderful view, over the water or over the land – whatever your heart desires.

In the evening, we find the time to experience the Sunday life of the "better" districts of the city. Merchandise stands, entertainment stands, a little children's amusement park – you can find everything here you would ever want. And on the street, which runs along the sea, there's a car race! It's probably only for the fun of the participants and the spectators, without any fees or prizes. No matter what their tastes, there are ways here for people to enjoy themselves! Early the next morning, we leave Naples, this time by bus. On the outskirts of the city, we pass the most primitive houses and dwellings, but soon we are traveling through beautiful countryside. Occasionally we drive through small villages that still show traces of the war. The inhabitants must be poor.

For a short stretch, the road follows the sea, but it's only a few hours before we reach the first houses of Rome. I am bombarded with many new names.

Some of them I have known for a long time, but that does not prevent me from getting them all mixed-up: St. Angel's Castle, the Tiber, the Vatican with the imposing dome of St. Peters, and, further off, the old ruins, some readily familiar, some less so. The Coliseum: when you see it, you feel goose pimples run over your back, as you imagine what all must have happened here. The bath, surrounded by dark cypresses, lets you feel the timelessness again. Here is peace.

However, there is no lack of modern buildings. The Eternal City! She seems to be entitled to bear this name. You have much to show me in Rome: the well-maintained park that is part of the Villa Borghese; the Chiesa Della Santa Maria Maggiore; a walk over the famous Spanish Steps, a favourite haunt of artists. It would take forever to see all there is to be seen in Rome, but our holidays need to include some rest, too. Therefore, on to the rocky coast of Livorno! There we will find peace; no one shall take it away – except, perhaps, the sea may be allowed to interrupt it.

The train carries us there overnight, and the next morning we step off, tired and hungry. It is grey and cold, and the bus leaves in two long hours. With eyes only half open and in need of some comfort, we soak in the view of the beautiful palm trees in front of the station. *(We still can do so – see the photo [not included]!)* Finally the bus comes to take us out of the grey city. However, out here every hotel shows a no-vacancy sign, and nobody wants to take us in. Dispirited, tired, and with aching stomachs we stroll along the seashore back to the city.

Now we feel a little better again, because the first rays of the sun are peeking between the branches of the trees and starting to warm us. Soon, it's finally late enough that it's not too early to present ourselves at Gioia's house to catch a little sleep. We've left enough time to walk to the rocky shore for a dip into the sea later, but this doesn't seem to be "our" holiday spot. With relief, we mount the train again, which takes us to La Spezia. Here we are luckier, and find a place for the night, where we rest up for our own quiet holidays in Portovenere. As soon as we can, on the afternoon of the following day, we take a boat out of La Spezia. After landing in Portovenere, we take possession of our room in the Locanda San Pietro. From there our first walk is to the seashore. A wonderful spot for swimming is lying there, just waiting for us. Finally.

But it's not only water that awaits us: after a long sleepy night we discover the other side of the peninsula, and the castle, surrounded by beautiful, delicately coloured olive trees. Steep, rocky trails lead to an incomparable viewpoint. Far down below the vertical rock cliffs is the sea. The little boats look like tiny dots. One can only look and look – at the unending horizon and the sea.

After this wonderful view, and full of the spirit of discovery, we start back down the mountain.

We also visit San Pietro, an ancient church steeped in legend. A handsome monk leads our tour, and explains that St. Peter himself had given the order for the church to be built.

This is the furthest tip of the island. And, look, through this rock gate you can get down to the sea and to Byron's Grotto. *(Photo [not included].)*

Also magical is a trip in a nutshell rowboat on the open sea, completely around the Island of Palmaria. For moments, big waves take away any view and you see only walls of water, but with his strong arms our boatman confidently brings us back into quieter waters, where we beg him to let us row, and he actually lets us. How varied in colour the sea can be! We are also shown how mussels are cultivated, the way these little animals hang by the thousands on stretched wires in the water. After the sunny afternoon on the sea, our boat returns quietly back to the Locanda San Pietro. It is our last evening, and for a long time we lean on the church wall and look at the waves. The illuminated boats of the fishermen float past in long rows, on their way out to set their nets. The dots of light grow smaller and smaller in the distance. It has been a while now since we have heard the noise of motors. Adieu, Portovenere! And many, many thanks!

In the freshness of the morning, the boat takes us back to La Spezia. Sunken ships and war-damaged houses await us there, but soon the train takes us away from them, by way of Genova, along the Riviera, hurrying on to Milano. Wonderful scenery "laughs" at us on all sides, but we are not entirely happy: it's the end of our holidays! One is not sure if one should be sad or happy for all that one has experienced. The latter is correct, of course, but in the rush of the moment the former is foremost.

Soon the train stops in Milan, where we leave it once more. After a short stroll, we find ourselves standing in front of the famous cathedral. One feels once again the peace and the coolness that emanates from these places. Only slowly does one turn to the large and beautiful works of art, both the hidden ones and those on bold display.

We do a little shopping, too, and soon we are sitting in the train again. It is late, so we spend the night in Domodossola. That way, we can see the area in the morning, our last one in Italy.

Before long, we reach the border. Customs! And there we change roles again. Now you are the guest, and I am at home! Here too, life is good to us, and we're both happy. These were two weeks in Paradise. And you were a very great travel guide; I thank you!

For Hugo from Dorothy
Christmas 1947

14. The Empress of France

After our interview with Mr. Watson of the C.P.R., Canada opened a legation on Thunstrasse in Bern. At that time, Canada was accepting immigrants from such former enemy countries as Italy, Hungary, and Romania, but not yet from Germany. Germans were only admitted again into Canada starting in 1952. As an Italian citizen, I was now certain I would acquire an immigration visa for permanent residence in Canada. This certainty gave me the confidence to get married and to plan a new life in Canada. We were married on October 16, 1948. By then, it had become possible to invite my parents to come – from a Germany devastated by the war – to my wedding in Switzerland, which the war had not touched. It must have been a very special experience for my parents, and especially for my mother, to attend our wedding in a country that was so normal and so different from her war-torn homeland. Not only did I arrange for my parents to attend the wedding, but also I arranged for them to travel to Italy, where they visited Roveredo in Piano. My mother had never been there. In fact, she had never even met any of the relatives.

The day after the wedding, Dorothy and I traveled to Bern, and on the next day, a Monday, we went to the Italian Legation and Consulate, where I used to work, to get a new Italian Passport for her, since by marrying me she had relinquished her Swiss citizenship and become Italian. Immediately after that, we left by train to Milan, where we had arranged to meet up with my parents, who had gone ahead. We all travelled together to Venice and then to Roveredo in Piano. The visit was a great success, especially for my mother, who had heard about these places and people for many years. My parents stayed on for a few more days, but right after the reunion Dorothy and I left to start our honeymoon. Who has ever heard of a newlywed couple making the first leg of their honeymoon in the company of their parents, or parents-in-law? Well, we had four weeks ahead, just for us, and we did not mind. On the contrary, we were very happy to have been able to offer such a great experience to my parents, especially after those five terrible war years of deprivation.

A relaxed holiday and honeymoon did not, however, start right away. First, we had to go to Sacile, my old military district, where I was supposed to collect the money I had earned as a POW. I still held a credit voucher for US $403, which the Italian Government owed me. It was two years since September 1945, when I had been discharged from the Army. At that time, the agreement had been that the Italian Government would honour our U.S. Dollar credit vouchers in Italian Lire. What they tried to do, however, was to give us the pre-war exchange rate of US$1 to 100 Lire, although in the meantime the exchange rate had drastically changed, to US$1 to 450 Lire. In 1945, an American officer had advised me not to exchange my credit voucher at this rate, but to wait until the Government would be forced to pay the current exchange rate. That is why I waited two years, and that newly re-valued money was what we now intended to use for our honeymoon.

When I presented myself in Sacile, however, I was told that the money would be released to me in about one month. We had a serious problem! Luckily, this problem was solved when I got in touch with a friend from Rome, Augusto Lucaferri, who had been with me in the POW camp. He, too, was due to collect his money – in his case, at the Military District of Rome. He collected it and lent me 180,000 Lire. I have never forgotten this great demonstration of friendship and trust.

Dorothy and I spent our almost four-week-long honeymoon in a hotel in Taormina, at the foot of Mount Etna in Sicily. Taormina was and still is the place where the world's upper class society congregates and vacations. It is as well known as Monte Carlo, the Italian Riviera, Rapallo, Portofino, and other popular destinations, and today it is flooded with artists and tourists.

Taormina is a very ancient town, founded by the Greeks before Christ was born. Even today the well-preserved ruins of the Greek amphitheatre overlook the sea from high above the town. Similar Greek ruins are found all over Sicily, which has been Greek, Roman, Carthaginian, Spanish, and finally Italian in 1860. Being at the foot of a live volcano, we wanted to go as close to the crater as possible. Sadly, although we were driven almost to the top, conditions were never good, and we didn't realize this dream. Several times, though, we hiked the long steep trail down to the sea, where we swam and sunbathed, before taking the fatiguing hike back up again.

The reason we stayed so long in Taormina was that it was illegal to export Italian Lire. Since I could not take them home to Switzerland but had to spend all my money in Italy, we had a wonderful time. We spent much time shopping and viewing the artistic displays of ceramics, jewelry and handicrafts. Dorothy was particularly impressed with the fine embroidered silk blouses there and bought one as a souvenir. Dorothy even bought some cloth and had a dress made, and I, too, added some items to my wardrobe. In 1947, there were no nightclubs or similar places of entertainment in Taormina, except movies, so we had to entertain ourselves, which one can guess is not difficult when you are on your honeymoon. The fine Sicilian cuisine of pasta in *brodo* (broth), pasta in *bianco* (white), and pasta *col sugo* (sauce) with vegetables and delicious fruits agreed with us, and in our hotel we were introduced to a fine desert or snack in the form of dried figs cut in half and filled with walnuts. We ate them daily. Just as it had been on the Isle of Capri, we were almost the only tourists there, partly because of the economy, but also because our visit was in the off-season. We passed the time on long walks, talking of our journey to Canada and wondering what it would be like to stay with Dorothy's uncle on a small island so far north of a big city. We looked forward to our adventure in a new land, so far away. At that time we believed that we would never come back to Europe to see any of our families, had accepted that fate, and emigrated willingly, but with a touch of sadness. And of course, we wondered what our life together would be like in a faraway country with only each other for support. Strangely, we never talked about children, but each probably thought of that possibility.

On our return to Switzerland, we stopped in Sacile to collect the money that was due to me. Fortunately, I did receive it this time, and could send the 180,000 Lire back to Augusto Lucaferri in Rome. To this day, I have kept the receipt stub from the post office.

Back in Hombrechtikon we had to wait for our Canadian immigration visa. During this waiting period I had to see if I could find a job, as I still needed to earn some money to support the both of us and to fill the waiting time. The wait wasn't too hard to bear, though, because although the length of our wait might have been uncertain, it was completely certain that the visas would be issued. I was fortunate to land a job in a bakery in Uetzikon about two kilometres from Hombrechtikon. To work there as a foreigner I needed a temporary work permit, which I had no trouble obtaining, although I had not worked in my trade during all the war years. I fitted in right away, baking bread Swiss style, and even baked some pastries. I worked there from November 1948 until we left Switzerland at the end of April 1949. When the Canadian Legation sent news that our visas were ready to be issued, we had our required medical examinations, and then decided to make one more trip to Germany, to say good-bye to my parents and to my brother and his family.

This last trip to Dalheim was rather eventful. At moments, it was even frightening. We had a French visa for ten days, from March 22, 1949 to April 23, 1949. Our problem was that at that time, in April 1949, one could not import German money into Germany. The reason was that you could change Swiss Franks into German Marks in Germany at a very unfavourable exchange rate, while in Switzerland your German Marks were sold for a far more favourable rate – almost ten times better, in fact. This situation was too tempting not to buy at least some German money in Switzerland. I bought only one fifty Mark bill, folded the bill very small, and put it in the very bottom of my coin purse. We went by train, and on the border into the French Occupation Zone the French Soldiers and guards checked us thoroughly. Of course, we did not declare the fifty Mark note I had hidden. Somehow, this one French customs officer must have had a sixth sense, or I must have shown great anxiety. After he had almost let us go back to the train, which was waiting for us, he called us back. Dorothy was subjected to a more thorough body check and once again I had to empty all my pockets and hand over my wallet and coin purse. This time, they found the fifty Mark bill. Because of that, the train was let go without us and we were questioned extensively, and then fined thirty American dollars, which I had on me and, fortunately, had declared. The fifty Mark note was confiscated. We were allowed to proceed on the next train – very late that night.

We finally reached Dalheim, but I do not recall when. Our visit was appreciated, but our good-byes were sad. In those days, to immigrate to "America" was to say good-bye forever. We were not financially in the class of people who could afford to make such long and costly ocean journeys more than once in a lifetime. After all, we did not emigrate in order to get rich, but rather for adventure and new life experiences. Dorothy had always wanted to go to Canada, because her cousin, Erica Hess, had her own horse to ride to school!

On our last night together, we went with my parents and my cousin Olga Gaab to see the opera *Rigoletto* in Wiesbaden. After the opera, we said our good-byes on the street: my parents went home to Dalheim, while we stayed the night at Olga's apartment in Wiesbaden. The apartment was temporary – she was living in it only because the American Occupation Forces had requisitioned her own undamaged and upper middle class house. To reassure my father, who was seventy-four at the time, I said, "In two or three years we will come back for a visit and see each other again." He just said calmly, "No, I don't think so," and he was right. He died the next year, in September 1950, of cancer of the throat. Apparently, as he was dying, he kept saying, "The same disease Caruso died of."

Back in Switzerland again, we went to Bern for our final medical examination – X-rays. When we presented the result of these to the lady at the Canadian Legation, Miss Scherf, she issued us the much-desired and long-awaited visa for permanent residence in Canada. When she saw that we were destined for British Columbia, where Henry Hess lived, she said: "You are going to the most beautiful and best province of Canada." We did not know it then, but we know now that she was right!

We left Hombrechtikon at the end of April and stopped in Basel to say good-bye to Dorothy's sister, Elisabeth Guex, her husband George, and their two daughters, Liselotte and Barbara, who was just a baby. Elisabeth gave us the address of a friend of hers in London, Irene, who gave us shelter for our three days there. From the train station we took a taxi to her address. Being unfamiliar with British currency, I thought I had tipped the driver properly when I paid the fare. The driver, however, just counted and sorted the money that I gave him and then threw a number of copper coins in the gutter and drove away without saying thank you! In London, we had no specific expectations and were impressed with the sites and the history that emanated from all we saw. In Madame Tussaud's Wax Cabinet was a wax figure dressed up as an attendant. It was stiff and lifeless, until after a few moments it started to fall over and turned out to be real and not a wax figure at all! In the Hall of Mirrors nearby we saw ourselves in all manners of distortions, and just about killed ourselves laughing.

We left by train for Liverpool, where, on the 3rd of May 1949, we embarked on the Canadian Pacific liner *Empress of France*, which had been a troop carrier during the war but had now been converted back into a modern passenger ship. It was an emotional moment, full of anticipation, when the 20,000-ton ship blew its horn and left the dock.

15. An Unexpected Haircut

*S*hips like ours were the first post-war passenger ships to resume service between Europe and North America. The passage across the Atlantic from Liverpool to Montreal, where we disembarked, lasted seven days and six nights, but our first stop in Canada was in Quebec City. Before we arrived there, a Canadian Immigration officer put a stamp in our passports that read: *Landed Immigrant, May 10, 1949.* Much later, it occurred to me that it was at that point that I closed the passport, put it back into my pocket, and never had to show it again anywhere to anybody in that big three-thousand-mile-wide country until six years later, in 1955, when we were about to receive our Canadian Citizenship papers. To me that was the ultimate evidence of real freedom, a freedom that did not exist in any of the countries we had left behind in Europe.

The seven-day voyage itself was uneventful, except that on the second-to-last day we had a Force-7 wind and most people did not show up for their meals. A British writer by the name of Edmonds told us we could avoid getting seasick by staying on deck and keeping our eyes on the horizon, which would always be steady. We did as he said, and it worked.

Among the people we met on the ship were a young Swiss German couple, Otto & Ruth Wüthrich, and a young Swiss bachelor, Paul Odermatt. We became good friends, and joined them for two months of the summer of 1950 in Fort St. John, B.C. Those three Swiss immigrants had little or no knowledge of English. When they had to select their meal from the elaborate menu, they couldn't understand the fancy names of menu items, so they just pointed at a variety of different things. The steward who politely took down their orders suppressed his astonishment about the combinations that resulted from their ad hoc choices. We noticed their surprise when their meals arrived, and since we sat at a nearby table we could not help laughing. Then, we laughed all together. From then on they consulted with us and we were able to translate some of the items on the menu for them.

Our first glance of the land that would be our new home was at the entrance to the St. Lawrence River. Although it was already the 10th of May there was still snow on the ground and the country looked desolate, uninhabited, and dead. When we saw that landscape, we took it for granted that we had arrived in Canada, where winter is longer, and that the apparent lack of population was one of the reasons why we were welcome as new immigrants. We just hoped that the part of British Columbia to which we were going would have a climate similar to the one we were used to in Switzerland, and hopefully would be more populated. In Quebec City, we were allowed to spend some time ashore. It was an exciting moment when we set foot for the first time in our new home country. We knew the language in Quebec was French. Because we both knew the language well, especially Dorothy, we were taken aback when we had difficulty communicating. We had a few hours to go on land and thought we could go to the city centre. Dorothy asked some people who were hanging around the port, *"Où se trouve le centre de la ville?"* She was not understood. It was the French pronunciation that was the difficulty, but to us it was the Québécois pronunciation that gave us trouble! I tried with English, but I had little success. After some concentrated effort, however, Dorothy managed it. It was quite an introduction to how different Quebec French is from that spoken in France and Switzerland.

During our short shore visit, we took a horse-drawn coach ride through the old city and admired the majestic Hotel Frontenac. After embarking again, we proceeded during the night to Montreal. We were booked on the C.P.R. train that same day, to ride across the entire three thousand miles of the country to Vancouver. In the spirit of our adventure, we were looking forward to the four nights and five days of the trip. However, while we were waiting for the scheduled departure, Dorothy saw a hair salon in the station and decided to get a haircut suitable for the farming she would soon be doing. While she was in the salon, I wandered around the station. When she was finished and came towards me I hardly recognized her! Her beautiful long brown hair was gone. Apparently, the stylist had not quite understood that she had wanted just a little bit cut off her hair. Instead, he had cut it so short that it almost looked like a man's haircut. He didn't mean badly, though. He just thought he was doing her a favour by giving her the latest modern style. It was a shock for both of us, but there was nothing we could do, except to wait for it to grow back. While we were dealing with this shock, our two Swiss friends also went to a barber for a shave. They, too, ran into a bit of a misunderstanding, and ended up not only with a shave but also with a total facial massage! They had not asked for it, but had enjoyed it anyway.

We had prearranged for a stopover at Dorothy's uncle's farm in Marsden, Saskatchewan. Because the train station for this lonesome prairie location was Artland, which was on the Canadian National rail line, we had to change trains from the C.P.R. to the C.N. in Saskatoon – the first city we had seen after Montreal. During the short wait for our connection, we stepped out of the station and saw at once the impressive C.P.R. Bessborough Hotel, right down the road. It was like many big hotels in Europe, a solid brick building with ornamental features to its appearance. It was impressive, because all the other buildings around it and on the main street were all just one or two stories high. We were reassured that Canada had more to offer than appeared on first glance. When we boarded the train again, we had to tell the conductor that we wanted to get off at Artland, because the transcontinental train did not normally stop at small mid-prairie stations like that.

In late afternoon, the train let us off with our baggage, and there we stood, in front of a single small building in the middle of nowhere, without a soul in sight. About a hundred meters away was what we assumed to be a farm building, but we saw no people anywhere. George Hiar, the man who was leasing Uncle Henry's farm and who was supposed to pick us up, was not there. We were all alone in the big wide Canadian prairie. It was then that we realized with a shock that all the round circles we had seen on Canadian maps while still in Europe, and which we had assumed were little towns and cities, as they were on the European maps we were used to, were in many cases only one, two or three houses, or even simply a location name. We were not too concerned, though: we figured someone would eventually show up. We sat down on our suitcases and waited, scanning the horizon to see if anything was moving anywhere – a car, or people, anything. After awhile, there was something. We saw a cloud of dust rising in the far distance, which we thought might be the sign of a car coming. Indeed, it was George Hiar, coming to pick us up and take us to his farm.

As the European relatives of Henry Hess, who had come from so far away to start a new life in Canada, we were treated like family. Of course, because we both spoke English, our adjustment caused no one any hardship, either! On Sunday, the Hiar family took us on a picnic, where we learned to sing "Cruising Down the River (On a Sunday Afternoon)." One Wednesday evening, we went with them to play whist in the community hall. Because neither of us knew the rules to whist, we kept asking each other questions about the game, in German – which the pair we were playing with found very upsetting. We quickly apologized and corrected our unintentional rudeness.

During the week or ten days we stayed in Marsden, we learned surprising things. Each winter men gather ice from the sloughs, pack it in sawdust, and store it in a dugout to have an "icebox" for the summer, and to keep milk and cream cold before delivering. Every year, on the 24th of May Victoria Day, the annual garden is planted – from then on, one hopes, there will be no more frost.

While on the farm, we were housed in a small but comfortable cabin. We also visited Uncle Henry's fine farmhouse. He had built it on a hill for its splendid view, like a good Swiss man would, but could not find a reliable source of water on that spot. The house did not resemble the typical prairie farmhouse but was rather like a Swiss chalet, although without the balcony and other Swiss ornaments, and not as big. Otherwise, though, it was a comfortable and beautiful home. I don't know how the water problem was eventually resolved.

At the end of our visit with the Hiars, we boarded the train again in Artland, for the trip to Vancouver, via Edmonton and Jasper. The views through the Rocky Mountains were spectacular. For us, it was like viewing the Alps, but magnified. In comparison with the Alps, the mountains were very rocky and covered with unending forests, with rarely a house or sign of human life or activity, and this went on for miles and miles. Despite having interrupted our cross-Canada journey with our stopover in Artland, we were still very impressed with the enormous distances we had crossed and the time it had taken to travel them. We felt overwhelmed and became slowly aware of what a big country we had come to. Even the train's passenger cars were bigger than those on European railroads. The seats reclined for sleeping and each car had a black steward who looked after you. It was all exciting for us and we were anxious to write home about it all.

After passing through Revelstoke and Kamloops, the train entered the Fraser Canyon. We were particularly taken with the Alexandra bridges, where the two railroads exchange sides by both crossing the Fraser River. Because the Canadian Pacific built the first line, they chose the easiest route, first on the east side of the canyon, and when that got too difficult, over to the west side of the river. Since the Canadian National came after, they had to use the route that was left, and had to cross the river – at the same spot! When we saw that, we asked ourselves why the two railway companies, the Canadian Pacific and the Canadian National, did not simply use the same track.

After such a spectacular voyage, our trip through the Fraser Valley, with its farms, towns and villages, was more like traveling through Europe, except that the buildings were quite different and the farms and the herds were much larger than those in Europe. In the afternoon we arrived in Vancouver, where Dorothy's Uncle Henry welcomed us. It was the first time we'd met – previously, we had only known each other through letters. He took us to his hotel, the Alcazar, on Pender Street, to deposit our luggage. Because it was the Victoria Day holiday, he then took us to a rodeo. This was something we had never heard of, nor ever seen, nor even imagined, with its absolutely stunning activities – bucking bronco riding, bull riding, and calf roping. While we experienced this sport for the first time, we thought the men were very courageous. Dorothy enjoyed the new experience, but said that that was not how she would use the horse she had always dreamed of having, when she finally got one!

We stayed about a week in the hotel. Henry took us to Chinatown for a Chinese meal – our first ever. When we saw people eating with chopsticks, we just had to try it. The food was so different from what we were used to, but it tasted delicious. We also visited Henry's daughter, Erica, who was in the hospital to have her first baby, and went with Henry to buy a cow and a cream separator to take to his home on Read Island, where we would live with him. One hundred thirty miles north of Vancouver, Read Island had very few inhabitants, mainly fishermen, who lived mostly along the water.

After Henry had arranged for the transportation of the cow and all the other goods he had purchased, we embarked on the Union Steamship Company's *SS Chelohsin* for a two-day and one-night trip. It took so long because this boat was the only supply line to some of the ports along the fjords of the west coast and stopped at them all. The journey was unforgettable, including the distances between ports and the scarcity of people along the entire route. The further north we travelled, the fewer people were at the docks to welcome the arrival of the boat and to receive the goods that were unloaded. Before nightfall of the second day, we arrived on the dock at Surge Narrows, the post office address for our island. Besides Mr. Tipton's General Store and Mr. Frost's Post Office, there were only a very few buildings, and about seventy-two people on the whole island. Surge Narrows Post Office was on the west side of the island; Read Island, the other post office, was on the east side. All our goods, including the cow, were unloaded and deposited on the dock, and from there we watched the ship leave for its next port of call.

Uncle Henry's house was about a mile inland through the forest from the dock, but it was a shorter trip by rowing a boat a short stretch along the shore, then following a quarter-mile-long path – also through the forest. His house was one of very few houses built away from the shore.   Getting the luggage to the house presented some problems. We had to carry the luggage, including a heavy overseas trunk, from the high dock down into a small rowboat. The trunk was quite heavy, and we came very close to losing our balance and dropping it into the sea. Then there was the cow! All this time, night had been falling, so Henry decided that I would lead the cow along the forest path. On the dock was a girl Henry knew, twelve or fourteen years old, by the name of June. She was to show me the way. So, there I was, just arrived from the modern, ultra-civilized cities and villages of Switzerland, to this "out of this world," forested island, only to be confronted with a cow, to have to lead it through a dark, unknown, unfamiliar forest, accompanied by a complete stranger, while my new wife and her uncle were somewhere in a small rowboat on the water, with our entire luggage! It was now that I could prove to myself that my adventurous spirit was alive and well.

It was. I proudly led that cow a mile through the huge cedar trees of that dense forest, when suddenly, not very far away, I saw a huge white object in the dark. I started, until June, who was patiently showing me the way, said, "Oh, that is only Pointrass' horse. He is always here!" Well, let's just say we got to the house, with our cow, and without any further surprises. The others were already there, but the luggage was still down on the beach. We would have to haul it up the next day with a wheelbarrow.

Uncle Henry's house sat on a slight elevation, in a clearing, with some rocks for steps to the front door. For fire protection, the sides of the house were covered with plates of tin. There was no electricity, no running water, and no telephone. The only thing that kept us up-to-date was the battery-powered radio. We got our water from a deep well. Set off at a little distance was the outhouse. Our sleeping quarters were under the sloping roof in the unfinished attic. This very simple pioneer lifestyle was certainly a contrast to the one we had come from. Our bed had old metal springs, which squeaked and rattled whenever one of us moved. Henry, who slept in the room below us, and who, at his age slept very lightly, knocked at the ceiling with a broom whenever he heard noises from upstairs.

According to the Canadian immigration visa, which admitted us as farmers, Uncle Henry was our sponsor, which meant that he had to guarantee us work on his farm for one year. After that, we could work anywhere else, as long as we worked for one year on a farm. A few days after we arrived in Surge Narrows we discussed the matter with him. In our letters, we had not made any arrangements regarding our stay with him or about finding work. He listened to our explanations, then he proposed the following solution: we would stay with him on the island for one year; Dorothy would do the housework, while I would help with all the odd jobs that needed to be done in such a pioneering situation – falling huge trees, building sheds, splitting cedar shingles, clearing more land for a garden, hauling sand by rowboat from another island for some cement work, clearing the quarter-mile-long path to the water, looking after the cow (which Dorothy had to milk, as that was part of the housework), and whatever else Henry saw as necessary. This was mostly non-profitable work, strictly for the maintenance and improvement of the place. For this, we would have room (as described earlier) and board, but it would not be a rigorous forty-eight hour workweek. We would take it easy, work when necessary, and, when we felt like it go on the odd excursion on the island or on neighbouring islands. For that, we would receive a combined salary of $150 at the end of the year. However, if we wanted more money, we could work a regular forty-eight-hour week, and receive $300 at the end of the year.

Well, we asked for time to think about this preposition, as we had no idea what the going rates for this type of work were. When Dorothy and I were alone and discussed the proposal, I was prepared to accept any conditions without thinking too much about them, but Dorothy had her reservations. To do housework under those conditions and circumstances would be very hard, she explained. To milk the cow, to do the cooking, make the bread, do the laundry for three, work in the garden, and do housecleaning, without tools like a vacuum cleaner, and to clean the coarse wooden floors, too, was all difficult for someone who came from an office job. Although the washing machine was gas-powered and quite "modern," to wash clothes with it Dorothy would have to fetch the water from the well, bring it in the house to heat it up, then take it back outside to the washing machine. It would all be very difficult. In the end, though, we agreed to the year's work for $150.

I had a rather scary experience while working for Henry. He wanted to build a shed with cement foundations, but because there was no sand on the shore to which we had access we had to haul it across from a neighbouring island. In two separate boats, we rowed over to the other island, Maurelle Island, which was north of Read Island and just across the water from Henry's section of 640 acres of forest. Henry used a regular clinker boat and I had a flat-bottomed ten-foot rowboat. As this was where the "surge narrows," so to speak, we had to pay great attention to the tide. We had to go with it to the place where the sand was and return with the loaded boots on the return tide, and to do all that we had to row around one smaller island and at one particular point row hard to break away from the current. If we did not make it, the tide would take us a long distance through a very narrow channel with a very strong surge, and then we'd have to row back from there, with all that heavy sand in the boat. Well, as it happened, we left our loading place a little too late: Henry, who had the lighter boat, made the breakaway at the critical spot, while I could not. In that flimsy, overloaded boat I was carried through the narrow passage by the strong tide. It was a terrifying experience. I'll never forget the bobbing of that boat with all the sand in it. If it had capsized there would have been no hope for me, because those waters are so cold that a person would last only a few minutes.

Once a week, the *Chelohsin* brought mail and supplies – whatever people had ordered from Eatons or any other store in Vancouver. That was the adventure on Read Island! The rest of the time we lived almost alone in nature. As beautiful as the sea was, it was extraordinarily cold. Our shore access was rocky. In July we did go in for a swim, but only briefly, to cool off. Some times we went to the shore, where we often saw seals and occasionally even whales. There was no sandy beach where we could dig clams or oysters, but we did pick loganberries and gather Labrador tea. We had to look out for devil's club, and fight the "no see'ems," those tiny black flies whose bite is worse than mosquito bites, but which you cannot see or feel until they have bitten you. These were all new experiences, which added to our adventure, especially since everything happened so soon after we had left "civilized" Europe.

After we had been with Henry for a few months, he left us alone for a couple of weeks, while he took a holiday in California. During that time, we really lived the romantic life. We also met another couple, Silvia and Bob Hunter, who lived on the shore of the island during the summer. When we discussed our arrangement with Uncle Henry, they were surprised that he had offered us so little. After that, we read advertisements in the Vancouver papers for couples as "steady help" on farms in the Lower Mainland: they were offered a dwelling to live in, board, and $150 a month, not a year! When we realized the situation, Dorothy felt we could not stay with Henry for a whole year earning nothing, because we would spend more than $150 during the year for clothes and supplies for our private use. She explained that the rough work I was doing was hard on jeans, shirts and shoes, for example, and because there was no barber on the island we had to buy a hair clipper so that Dorothy could cut my hair. I agreed with everything Dorothy said.

When Uncle Henry came back, Dorothy found the courage to mention our decision not to stay a year with him on the island but rather to look for another job on the Mainland. Uncle Henry was not too upset, only a little annoyed that he had bought that cow, because, although it was a good idea for the three of us, it was impractical for him to keep just for himself. Nevertheless, he was understanding, and said he would give us $150 for the three months we had already spent with him. He suggested we go to the Okanagan Valley, a fruit-growing area. Because we were vegetarians, we did not want to work on a farm where animals were raised for slaughterhouses, be they chickens, pigs or cattle, so the thought of fruit farming appealed to us very much. We thanked Henry, said our good-byes and took the next boat to Vancouver. After a week in the Marshall Hotel for $3 a night, we took the C.P.R. to Penticton via the Coquihalla route. We arrived at Penticton's Hastings Street Station early in the morning of September 7, 1949.

When we came to Penticton, it had a population of less than 6000, mostly farmers who had fruit orchards. The main street was gravel. Part of it still had wooden sidewalks and thick power posts. The buildings on Main Street had false fronts like in many old western towns. Saturday nights, the stores were open till 9:00 o'clock, to give the farmers time to do their weekly shopping and to go to the beer parlour, which was divided for "Gents" and "Ladies and Escorts." Coming from Europe as we did, the B.C. Liquor Law and the Lord's Day Act really puzzled us. On Sundays, no restaurant was allowed to serve wine or beer, and sport games and movies were not allowed. Since I had decided not to drink wine or beer any more either, I did not miss those things. There was a Government Liquor Store with only a small selection of wines. A bottle of Australian Cavarra Riesling was $1.25; I would have had to work two hours at sixty-five cents an hour to buy a single bottle!

16. Popular Photography

After our arrival on that September morning, we left our luggage at the train station and walked about a mile to the Farm Labour Office on the shores of Okanagan Lake. We carried a letter from the C.P.R. Agent in Zurich, Mr. Watson, who recommended us and indicated that we had immigrated with the intention of becoming farmers in Canada. When we came in to the office, one of Penticton's orchardists, Mr. Arthur Pearson, was already there, looking for fruit pickers. When he saw us and read the letter of recommendation, he hired us on the spot. After driving us to the station to pick up our luggage, he took us to his orchard, about five miles out of town on the Naramata Road. That early September morning ride was our first, and most unforgettable, impression of another Canada, the Okanagan. It sure was different from the giant trees and the dense forests of the Pacific Coast! We drove the entire trip through orchards. To the right and the left of the road, trees were laden with fruit waiting to be picked: apples, pears, prunes, and peaches. When Mr. Pearson turned off the main road onto the private road down to the lake through his orchard, he stopped to let us get out and pick up some of the ripe peaches on the ground. We were astonished to see so much good ripe fruit wasted, while the main crop of the tree was still waiting to be picked. On our way through the orchard we also saw our first coyote crossing the road.

We settled into a drafty little old boathouse. Outside our door, the lake was still warm enough to go swimming. There was no running water and no electricity, but primitive as it was this accommodation suited us fine, despite the fact that during the night we could hear the pack rats running around – some of them even over us! We didn't mind. It was part of the adventure of adapting to a new country and a new life.

However, we could stay there for only a couple of weeks. When it grew too cold, we had to move farther up the orchard to a picker's cabin, which had heat and a stove for cooking our meals. Even though it was better equipped for living, with electricity and running water, we were not as happy there as we had been in our little boathouse on the beach.

Our working arrangements gave us free rent for the cabin. For our labour itself, we were paid by the hour: Dorothy received fifty cents and I received sixty-five cents an hour picking fruit. We soon got used to our new jobs and did quite well. When I heard from other pickers that one could pick the apples by the box, and receive ten cents a box, I asked the owner's son, Bob, who ran the orchard (his father was the city engineer), if we could pick that way. He said "Sure! Tomorrow you may pick by the box." We learned a lot that day. Whereas up to that time we had been put on smaller, richly-loaded trees, with ten-foot ladders, and therefore filled many boxes in our ten hour day, we now were assigned to big tall trees, with heavy fourteen- and sixteen-foot-tall ladders. Because these were trees with an off-year crop, we picked half as many boxes of apples, and earned about half as much money as when we had worked by the hour just the day before. After this one-day experience, I gathered the courage to ask Bob if we could pick by the hour again. He said yes, and the next day we were back on the lower trees, with shorter and lighter ladders.

During those first few weeks, we had the opportunity to meet some of the neighbour orchardists. The first was Harry Bermbach and his two children, Barbara and Bernie. Harry had come from Germany in 1928 – as it turned out, from Kronberg im Taunus, just a few kilometres from Wiesbaden. Meeting him was a lucky coincidence for us, because he introduced us to other German immigrant families with orchards, who also had come to the valley in 1928. One of those was the Grundig family, Alfred and Tilly and their two teen-age sons, Frank and Jürgen. We were fortunate to meet this particular group of Germans, because the Canadian authorities knew them as the "good" Germans, who were not Nazi sympathizers. There were others in the Valley, who were sympathizers. During the war, those Germans had been required to report regularly to the authorities, whereas the ones we had met had only reported once a year for the duration of the war. Many of the Germans we met were adventurous and idealistic – young men and women who had left Germany in 1928, when life in Germany began to get better after the post-WWI years. At first only a very few came to the Okanagan, but when they realized the opportunities that were open to them they invited many of their friends. Each of those invited some more, and the movement swelled. They started out as a commune, buying land together for orchards, and made a living that way. Eventually, the commune broke up and just about every one of these Germans acquired his own orchard. That is how we found them. Some had left good professions: Pruesse had been a banker, Grundig a fine mechanic, Schwenk, I believe, a teacher. Most of them had a trade. They did not, however, want to have anything to do with Germany any more and adapted well and willingly to the Canadian way of life.

Because Dorothy and I both spoke English, we did not feel very much like immigrants. Even our German accents did not create any hostility so soon after the end of the war. Only one time did someone call me, disparagingly, "You D.P.!" (Displaced Person), so I agreed with him and said "Yes, we are Delayed Pioneers." In general, though, I never felt like an immigrant, nor was I ever treated like one in a negative way. We are forever thankful to Canada: it gave me a life I could never have had in Europe, with its class system and the papers you needed to have to do something or to be somebody.

Little did I know then, however, that my introduction to the Grundigs would shape my future in Canada. Besides running his orchard, Alfred was also an artist. He painted, sculpted, made fine furniture, was a draftsman, a fine mechanic and an amateur photographer. He had a darkroom, where he developed his films and made black and white prints.

While working for Mr. Pearson, we also worked on odd days for other orchardists in the neighbourhood. After the harvest was completed at the end of October though, we could no longer stay in Mr. Pearson's cabin, since he no longer had any work for us. This was no problem: we moved into a cabin on the upper part of the Grundigs' orchard. It was very nicely finished on the inside, but was not insulated. It was about twelve feet by sixteen feet, and was divided in the middle to make two rooms. One served as both the kitchen and living room. The other, smaller one was the bedroom. There was a good kitchen woodstove, but no electricity or running water. The toilet was about fifty meters away on a beautiful spot. When you left the door open, you had a fantastic view of Penticton in the distance, the valley, Okanagan Lake, and the surrounding mountains. We had to fetch our water from a spring about seventy-five meters from our door. The cabin was situated next to the irrigation flume, which, up until harvest time, carried water to irrigate the orchards. During the time that the water was running, we had it right outside our door. Before it was shut off for the winter, however, the farmers had to fill their cisterns, which had to last them until the water was turned on again in the spring.

We rented this cabin for $7 a month. By doing one ten-hour day of work for Mr. Grundig, our rent for the month was paid. We became very good friends with the Grundigs, who more or less adopted us. They were extremely helpful and introduced us to many fine people in Penticton, Summerland and Osoyoos, all friends of theirs, who in turn became our long-lasting friends as well. How protective the Grundigs were can be illustrated by the following incident. When I had applied for a Shell gas credit card and was asked for a reference, I gave Alfred Grundig's name, knowing that he would vouch for my honesty and reliability. Unfortunately, I forgot to mention this to Alfred. When the Shell people phoned him and asked about me, he said he did not know me. When I saw him the next time, he mentioned that some people had phoned him and had asked him all kinds of questions about me, but because he thought they had no business asking all kinds of personal questions about me, he had told them that he did not know me.

At the end of the picking season, I had no more work in the orchards, but because we paid so little rent and we had a bit of a savings account – $2000 which we had brought with us to Canada – we did not worry, and looked forward to our first winter in Canada. We intended to use our savings as a down payment for a fruit farm of our own. We actually had an eye on one, belonging to a Swiss orchardist, Mr. Karrer. At that time you could buy a ten-acre apricot orchard, with a proper house on it, for $10,000, so we had enough for a down payment.

As Christmas approached, we were told the winter in the Okanagan is always very mild, with little snow or cold. We were told it might get as cold as 14° Fahrenheit (10° Celsius), but no colder. On December 17, 1949 we saw the first snow in the valley. It was not very cold. We had a white Christmas and celebrated with the Grundigs on Christmas Eve, in keeping with our European tradition – with the usual exchange of little gifts and the singing of traditional German Christmas carols. For New Year's Eve, or *Sylvester*, as we call it in German, we were invited to join the Grundigs and their friends for a New Year's party. In their spacious living room we danced, and in the basement we did the traditional Blei giessen: we poured molten lead into a bucket of cold water, then interpreted the resulting configurations as predictions for the coming year. Dorothy and I were pleased to be accepted as newcomers and part of this group of kind people. The party went on until almost 6:00 in the morning, when we finally walked back to our "cozy" cabin. It seemed rather cold, but it was winter, after all, and we went straight to bed without giving it a further thought. After a good sleep, we woke up around 2:00 o'clock in the afternoon and got up to start our day, the 1st of January 1950. To our surprise, everything liquid in the cabin was solidly frozen: the water, the milk, the ink, the fruit, the vegetables – everything. The cold had started that night, and lasted until February 6. The thermometer soon went down to minus 17° Fahrenheit (minus 27° Celsius). Slowly, both Skaha Lake and Okanagan Lake froze solid. The barges, which brought C.P.R. and C.N. freight cars from Kelowna to Penticton, could no longer break through the ice and the ferries, which at that time were the only connection across the lake between Kelowna and Westbank, also froze in. Our uninsulated cabin was very cold, and the heat from the kitchen stove was not effective at keeping us warm. Going to our windswept outhouse was an especially rough experience. Another tough chore was getting water from the spring – at least it kept running! To walk about seventy-five meters through snow and ice with two buckets of water was not easy. We bought a load of slap wood from the Leir Sawmill to burn in our kitchen stove, but soon discovered that old, thick tree bark burned longer and gave lots of heat – although it also gave a lot of soot. After that, we went into the hills behind our cabin to collect bark for our kitchen stove. All these hardships did not bother us. On the contrary, we saw them as adventures, and had lots to write home about!

During this time Dorothy wrote several reports home, and published others in Swiss publications. They accepted and published her articles about a young emigrated couple's experiences in their new homeland. For entertainment we bought a portable, battery operated General Electric radio for sixty-five dollars. A replacement battery cost twenty-two dollars. Penticton's new radio station, CKOK 800, was just one year old. It broadcast mostly advertising (which was, of course, the reason for its existence) and popular music. Only for one hour a day, between 2:00 and 3:00 o'clock, did it air a little classical music. We missed music like that. Finally, we discovered that we could tune into a station in San Mateo, California, which gave us many hours of enjoyment.

We spent many of the chilly evenings of that long, cold winter at the Grundigs', playing cards, chess and table tennis in their big living room. We were often invited to have supper with them. It was during those after-dinner evenings that Alfred Grundig introduced me to photography. He took me into his darkroom and showed me how a beautiful picture could appear on a blank sheet of photographic paper after it had been exposed to light through a negative in the enlarger and then put into a solution. The process fascinated me, and Alfred and I talked at length about cameras and photographs. We read *Popular Photography*, and I was thoroughly bitten by the photography bug. From then on, my little Italian-made *Ferrania* box camera wouldn't do any more! For $49.95, I bought an *Argoflex*, an American-built twin lens reflex camera, from Stocks Camera Shop. It took medium format 620-size film for 6x6 cm negatives. With this camera, I started to take photographs, which I developed and printed in Alfred's darkroom. In photo magazines, Alfred and I saw invitations to submit photographs for acceptance by the salons of different camera clubs. Four prints could be submitted, mounted on 16x20 inch boards. On my suggestion, Alfred agreed that we should each submit four prints to the Edmonton Cross Road Camera Club. How surprised and pleased I was when I had two of my prints accepted and Alfred only one! It certainly was a great encouragement to continue with my chosen hobby. After that success, I continued to submit photographs to various salons, and had some accepted in Canada, the U.S.A., Italy, Luxembourg and other places. After photography became my hobby, I wondered if it could become a job, but I was not sure, since when I mentioned it to Alfred Grundig, he told me "You need to go to an art school to become professional!" However, I kept doing what I was doing, and lived from day to day with a very tolerant and supportive wife. I cruised the Okanagan Valley and its side roads extensively, looking for pleasing and, if possible, unique images. Dorothy, and later the children, were always with me (I needed them as models in some photographs.) It was entertaining for them, and they were continuously exposed to the outdoors and the beautiful country of the Okanagan.

On the 6th of February 1950, the cold weather changed into early spring and the orchardists started to prune their trees. That is when they discovered that their fears of considerable frost damage to the trees had come true – especially to all the soft fruit trees, like apricots, cherries, peaches and prunes, but also to some pears and apples. Still, the surviving trees had to be pruned anyway. On the morning of that 6th of February Mr. Karrer came to ask me if I wanted to learn to prune trees and work for him. I think it's likely that he came to look for me because he knew my wife was Swiss and he was trying to help us, in a good Swiss way. From him, I learned to prune trees, and had work again. It was, however, easy to see that because of the frost damage this job would not last through the summer: with all the soft fruit frozen, no orchardist would need steady help during the year. Since we wanted to buy a fruit farm anyway, I decided I would work in our own orchard. With this plan in mind, Dorothy and I went to the Royal Bank of Canada, where we had our savings, and asked for a loan. Our plan was to borrow $8000 to buy Mr. Karrer's ten-acre orchard, along with its house, and pay it off with each year's crop. So we went to see the bank manager, Dick Duncan. The first thing he asked us when we said we wanted to take out a loan was whether we had any cash. When we said we had $2000, he said, "Sure you can get a loan. How much do you need and what do you want it for?" When we told him we wanted to buy an apricot orchard, he just laughed and said, "I'll give you a loan for anything except for an orchard, because for the next few years you will have no crop and will not be able to make any payments on your loan." That was the end of our dream.

After everyone we knew and met told us that there would be no work in the fruit industry that year, we decided to buy a vehicle and drive north to Fort St. John, where the Swiss friends we had met on the boat had taken up farming. We planned to look for work there, since our friends had indicated that lots of jobs were available in that area.

With that in mind, we went out to buy a vehicle. We did not want to buy a used one, because we knew nothing about cars: by buying a new one we could be sure we would not have any trouble with it. We went to Valley Motors and looked at new cars. We felt that the best thing for us would be something like a van, in which we could sleep. The salesman showed us a "Thames" closed panel truck, a British Ford, for $1100, and we bought it. There went half of our savings! Since neither Dorothy nor I could drive, the salesman kindly offered to teach us what we needed to know, so we quickly went to the Provincial Court House, where we each bought a driver's license for one dollar. The clerk told us that we would be advised by mail when an examiner from Victoria would come to give us our driver's test. With our new licenses in our pockets, we went back to the car salesman to pick up our new car. In our new car, he took us on a muddy country road on the Indian Reserve. There he showed me how to drive, and how to start the engine with the optional hand crank if the ignition did not work. I had to learn how to use the choke and how to shift gears with the clutch. In those days, one still had to double clutch, which was a tricky thing if you had never done it before. Well, I tried, but stalled the engine a few times. However, the salesman thought that I did well enough for a first time. He drove us part way along the Naramata Road and let us drive home alone, another three miles. For better or worse, there we were with our new car and our driver's licenses. Of course, I was unperturbed. I was sure I could handle this situation easily!

On my first attempt to drive alone, however, the engine stalled as I was going into first gear. When I tried once more, the engine stalled again. This went on a few more times. With utmost patience, Dorothy watched me without saying a word. She had faith in me, and thought I would manage in the end. However, after so many failures, she finally asked me, "May I give it a try?"

"Sure," I said, not believing that she could do any better. That was very foolish. Dorothy took the wheel, went into first gear, let the clutch go slowly at the friction point, and to my surprise and considerable humiliation the car moved forward at the first try. That same night, fifteen-year-old George Grundig taught me about the friction point. In the next few days we drove a few times to a vacant lot in Naramata, where we practiced starting and changing gears until we were properly familiar with our new car.

I worked on the orchards until the beginning of May. On May 20, the very day we had set for leaving Penticton for Fort St. John, we received notice in the mail to report in a few days for our driver's examination. I advised the examiner's office that we were just leaving for Fort St. John and that I would inform them after our return from this trip. We left, and after three thousand miles of driving behind us returned to Penticton and were ready to take the driver's examination, which of course, we passed.

17. We Immigrated to Canada as Newlyweds – Dorothy's Swiss Article on Our New Life

We got married with nothing. A *Hermes-Baby*, a pile of books, a few pieces of clothing, and three suitcases we could call our own, but a dowry – consisting of furniture, bed and kitchen linen, and the countless little things which fill a household, and which are often even considered essential for setting up a home at all – well, we had none of those. There wasn't much money in our pockets, either.

But in its place we possessed something quite different, something of exceptional value, namely an immigration visa for Canada and the necessary train and steamer tickets to go with it. And once you get there? And whatever are you going to do there? Are you going to live in sleeping bags in a tent?

But what can life offer you if you know everything before you even start? Prepared for the worst and excited by every new experience, we landed in our enormous new country.

My husband is an office clerk by trade, and very talented with languages. My own education was as a salesgirl, followed by two years experience as a secretary. And when we arrived in Canada, we got to choose: city, wilderness isolation, or the golden mean. We decided on the latter. At the labour office, which we visited as soon as we arrived, we were both snapped up within minutes by a farmer, who drove us off in his car to work on his orchard.

He suggested that we buy our first week's food – everything we'd need to live on – before we left town for the farm. Did we have money to pay for it with?

Before we knew it, he drove us to the grocery store, where we could buy "everything." I examined all the shelves of the store carefully, and put the likeliest articles in my basket. I didn't have much time for painting myself a picture of the home that was waiting for us. The only thought there was time for as I pushed everything mechanically through the till, was, "How American!" In the end, though, our things were paid for, loaded into the car, and we drove with anticipation towards our new home.

After a half-hour drive, the car turned into a side lane, drove down the cliff to the lake, and stopped on a little lawn in front of a boathouse. We were excited: so close to the water? Beautiful! One wall of the green-painted cabin swung open and gave an unobstructed view of the lake – through a screen – and into the mountains across the water. "Get yourselves settled, and if you need anything else ask my daughter-in-law. She might be able to help you," said the boss as he drove off, and we were left to contemplate our new home. In the middle of the room (there was only one), there was an iron bunk bed – army surplus from the Army & Navy store. On the top and the bottom there were two mattresses and one pillow, whose pink, shimmering silk cover spoke of a nobler origin. In the darkest corner there was a small stove, and on the counter next to it a little gas cooker. There were many shelves in the room, enough to make many housewives jealous of us, but for our few things we didn't need all of them in the least! There was a table close by, too, and two chairs, and even something resembling an ice cooler: a chest with thick wooden walls, covered in hammered tin, in which you put ice, on which you could store your groceries. There was even a mirror hanging on the wall, and next to it a cooking pot and a frying pan.

Our first home! In order to get a better look at everything, and to have a better handle on what we had got ourselves into, we started in right away, sweeping out the sand, dust and mouse droppings, under which a good linoleum floor gradually came to light. Soon, everything was set up, just as we wanted it – a house right on the lakeshore, what more could anyone ask for? Swimming and eating, work (as fruit pickers) – swimming and eating, work – swimming and eating, work – swimming and eating, and then crawling into our sleeping bags and leaving the barracks to the mice: our daily life.

But before long, the cool, damp autumn nights drove us out of our summer residence. Our suitcases were hauled up the mountain by the tractor and unloaded in front of a square little cabin, which was going to be our home for the autumn. The farmer gave us this place free of charge, too, as long as we continued to work on his farm. Exhausted from the hard work of the previous week, we stepped into our second home and – Oh no! – tears flooded our eyes and rolled down our cheeks. Pictures of our old home in Switzerland rose up before our eyes – but we soon screwed up our courage again. Really, a dozen beautifully crocheted linen tablecloths wouldn't have been of any use to us there! If we had brought them along, we would just have had to continually haul them around – unusable and unused frills!

Fetch water and scrub the cabin down, carry everything outside and only take back into the clean cabin what is more-or-less usable – and around midnight, our home was ready for us to move in. Even so, this solidly built, isolated little wooden shack, with its two narrow little windows, consisted of just one, single room. The rough wooden walls were blackened with soot, and the glaring light of the benzene lamp threw out ghostly shadows. The set-up was much like that in the boathouse: stove, built-in counter, table, two chairs, and a bed. Our suitcases filled up the rest of the space – and we were snug at home again.

That was how we got started – pretty normal for around here. We didn't need to pay any rent, as long as we worked for the owners of the cabin. And then, when our work came to end with the start of the winter, we had saved up enough to rent a prettier cabin. This one, too, was furnished with only the bare essentials. Well, that meant that we could begin to buy our own household things at our own pace. There was a good stove (which also served as a heater). We bought some cutlery, bed linen, a radio, and – a car. You come across so many dilapidated shacks here, from which people step out in lovely clothes, climb into a gleaming new car, and drive to see a movie. The way they see it is: most importantly, a person has to live properly before he gets weighed down with the huge financial burden of a house and gets tied down to one place forever. A car is more important than good furniture; it makes you independent from the huge distances in this country. Just as important is a washing machine, almost more important than running water and electricity. Your furniture should be comfortable, even your kitchen, if you like. But the house, the shell for the whole thing – well, as long as it holds together!

And so you add one little piece onto the next, without having to go into debt. If you don't want your old things anymore, you let someone else who's just starting out use them, just as she will pass them on later in turn. Marry with little money, without a dowry – why not? As long as you have your health and there's work for the taking.

Dorothy Redivo-Vögeli

18. A Carpenter's Helper

Before we drove north, we asked the Grundigs if we could leave our belongings with them and move back into the cabin if and when we came back in the fall. They said we could, as long as someone else had not moved into it while we were gone.

Then we were off! Our first stop was at Alfred Gruhl's in Osoyoos – a friend of the Grundigs. We slept in our panel truck, but with all the things we were taking along it was very awkward. Just to have room to sleep, we had to re-arrange everything! When Alfred Gruhl saw the trouble we were having, he built us some shelves and installed them in the van for us. From then on going to bed at night was much easier.

Early the following morning, we headed east, up the Anarchist Mountain Road. At that time, that stretch of highway was still under construction – just to reach the start of the road we had to drive over a stretch of sand and gravel. Our Thames could not make it! It simply spun out in the sand. Two enterprising young men were parked right there with a jeep and for a fee they offered to pull us up to the road. We had no choice and paid their fee: $2. Once we were up on the highway, we soon found out that the steep grade uphill was all sand and gravel, too. We could only drive in first and second gear and had to stop often to let the motor cool and to add water – when we found some. By nightfall, we finally arrived near Rock Creek, forty miles from Osoyoos. It had taken us the whole day.

We parked in what we thought was a good camping spot near a little creek, but when we woke up in the morning our van was sitting in two inches of water: the little creek had risen quite a lot overnight. Our "fine parking lot" was actually a little swamp. We did not let it bother us, though: we put up our card table and chairs anyway and had breakfast right where we were. From Rock Creek, we crossed three passes through the Cascade Mountains, then the Kootenay Pass and the Crowsnest Pass, before we finally made it, days later, to Waterton Lakes National Park. We stopped whenever we felt like stopping and stayed overnight whenever we found a suitable place. It was a gypsy life.

The paved road lasted only fifty or sixty miles past Edmonton, then continued as a gravel road. After that it was just dirt. Because the roads were dry, there was a lot of dust. It settled in thick layers inside our van – we had to clean the whole van every night before we could even cook and eat. Finally, at Mile Zero of the Alaska Highway at Dawson Creek, we hit gravel again; fifty miles later, we were in Fort St. John, where we met up with Ruth and Otto Wüthrich and Paul Odermatt. They had settled on a lot near the town's small airport, where the Wüthrichs had started a dairy and were doing quite well. For the time being, we parked there and stayed in our van.

Otto had written to us that there were many different types of jobs available for the taking in Fort St. John. He told me that in a growing pioneer town like that, the booming construction trade needed carpenters badly, because few trained people were willing to live that far north. He suggested that I buy some tools, make myself a wooden toolbox, and offer my services as a carpenter to a contractor who was building houses near the airport. I did just as he said, and I was hired right away, too, for $2.50 an hour. On my first day, my employer, Mr. Dodds, instructed me to nail some shiplap on the ceiling of a room. Although I had never in my life done anything like that, I had enough common sense (and courage) to start nailing these boards very gingerly on the ceiling. I hammered each nail in with many little tap, tap, tap, taps. Mr. Dodds walked the floor back and forth in the room where I was working, watching me. He did not look very pleased and eventually lost his patience, jumped on the scaffold, took the hammer out of my hand, took a nail, and pounded it into the ceiling with two blows: TAP, TAP! Then he gave me back my hammer and said: "You are no carpenter, but you can keep working if you will be satisfied with carpenter's helper wages of $1.25 an hour." I accepted the proposition without hesitation, because it was just about double the sixty-five cents I had earned in the orchards. Dorothy got a job, too – housekeeping for a lawyer in town. Because there was no indoor plumbing, her most repulsive duty was to empty the man's chamber pot. She also worked for Mr. Dodds in his general store. There she had to learn to deal with the rough crowd of workers who came in to buy their supplies. Her knowledge of English was tested by their colloquial speech.

Having found jobs, we had to look for a place to live. The rent for a very simple place was a minimum of fifty dollars a month. We decided to buy a tent from Eatons for fifty dollars. The tent was 6x9 feet. It had a floor and was high enough to stand in. We lived in it from the end of June to the early days of September: two full months. We put it up on the Wüthrich's lot and were very comfortable. On the outside, on the shady side of the tent, we dug a hole where we kept our milk and other perishables cool. We were doing very well, until the 15th of August when we had a snowstorm. It lasted for two days and left two inches of snow on the tent. It was very cold, but we were able to heat the tent a little with our Coleman stove. After a few days, the snow disappeared again. This experience made us decide not to stay up north; we liked the climate of the Okanagan much better!

Because of the snow and the subsequent rain, the dirt roads south of Dawson Creek had all turned to mud and were not passable by smaller cars like ours. I drove daily to town to ask the drivers of big rigs, who had come into town from Edmonton, about the road conditions. They always asked, "What are you driving?" When I said, "A little Thames," they all laughed and said I would never get through to Edmonton until the roads were really dry.

It was on one of these trips to town that I had my first car accident. The road to town was gravel, good enough for regular highway speeds, but it was also crossed several times by dirt roads. Wherever farm vehicles crossed it with wet mud on their wheels, the mud dropped off and built up in a slippery layer on the gravel. Even though I slowed down before hitting the slippery spots, on one of them my van did not stay on the road but slipped slowly to the side and tipped over into the ditch. There were no seatbelts at that time, but I did not get hurt. I opened the door above me and climbed out.

It was discouraging to hear the same story every day: with my type of car I would not get through. As time went on, we grew impatient and decided to leave anyway. We would face whatever happened, when it happened. Fortunately, besides minor troubles, we got all the way through to Edmonton – this time without all the dust. It was a funny feeling suddenly to be traveling on paved roads again.

From Edmonton we drove west via Calgary, Banff, Lake Louise, and Golden. From Golden, we drove for two hundred miles along the Big Bend Highway to Revelstoke. The Big Bend (which no longer exists) was a long and unpredictable gravel road with only one gas station and a bit of a store at the halfway mark, and mosquitoes en masse, everywhere. On the new road through Rogers Pass, it is only ninety-one miles (148 kilometres) from Golden to Revelstoke.

We arrived in Revelstoke at night and were very happy to have made it, despite all the mosquito bites. The next day we drove all the way to Summerland, where we stayed with friends. We were happy to be back "home." Luckily for us, the frost damage to the trees had not been as severe as everyone had feared, so we were able to move back into our cabin and start picking apples again. The following winter was milder than our first winter, so I was able to work the whole winter in the orchards. The work in the orchard was very hard. I had to dig around trees to remove the couch grass that had grown there, so that the mice, which were hiding in the grass, would not get at the tree trunks. I had to kill them, too, which was a most disgusting part of that job. Besides working in the orchard, I spent a lot of time in Alfred Grundig's darkroom. Dorothy also became interested, and spent hours making prints there. What's more, the high school offered adult education classes. I took a course in woodworking, in which I made a practical little cabinet, following the directions in a copy of *Popular Mechanics* magazine. The cabinet is still part of the furniture in Dorothy's bedroom.

In the meantime, the year that we were required to work as farmers had expired. We did not celebrate, but from that day on we felt free, and felt that we could take on any job that was available to us. We did, however, file our intention to become Canadian citizens. The conditions at that time were that after two years in the country an immigrant had to declare his or her intention to become a citizen; three years later citizenship would be granted – after five years in Canada. When Dorothy and I received our citizenship papers in 1955, we became British subjects, not Canadian citizens. The Canadian Citizenship Act came later. My attitude about changing citizenship was that, although I would never have changed my nationality while living in Europe, since I was a permanent resident in Canada I felt an obligation to become a part of the country and to vote in elections.

One day a man came to see me while I was working in an orchard and offered me a job to work for a plasterer. Somehow he had heard that I had worked in the construction business with my father in Germany. As he offered me $1.25 an hour, which was much more than the seventy-five cents an hour I was getting in the orchard that winter, I accepted the job. Work there at Brown-Byer Plastering Contractors was physically harder work, but the extra earnings were welcome.

The rest of the year and the beginning of the next year I worked for the plastering company: mixing and carrying the mortar, or "mud" as it was called in the trade. This work was not very steady. Some days we worked and some days not. Therefore I looked for another job, but with similar pay. Looking through the Vancouver Sun classifieds, I saw an ad for a firm looking for a terrazzo and cement worker. Since I had worked in my father's terrazzo and cement business in Germany, first occasionally and then for one full year, I felt qualified to apply. I mailed in my application, and soon after received a telegram that I was hired and could begin working right away.

The first job was in Vernon, seventy-five miles (120 kilometres) north of Penticton, where the boss's son had a contract to lay a terrazzo floor in the new Liquor Store. I was to report there the next day. My pay would be $1.25 an hour, plus meals and lodging while I was there. The job lasted a couple of weeks. I enjoyed the work, because I knew it well and because I was better paid than in the orchard. Vernon was a town very much like Penticton, except that it had a different layout and the train came right through town. I missed Dorothy: it was the first time we were apart since we had married. On the first weekend she came by Greyhound bus to visit me. In her diary on that day she entered, "Poor Hugo has to work four hours to pay for this bus ticket!" This was in March. It was still winter, and, although it was less severe than our first winter in the Okanagan, Skaha Lake was still solidly frozen over.

The job in construction was very promising, so in the spring of 1951 we moved to Vancouver. Again, we left most of our belongings with the Grundigs

– in case the job in Vancouver did not pan out, as the saying goes. It didn't. It was the same as with the plastering job in Penticton: two or three days work a week, and the other days waiting to be called.

On our arrival in Vancouver we were able to rent an apartment, for forty dollars a month, on Selkirk Street, very close to where the boss lived, Mr. Bruno, an Italian Swiss from Tessin. Every morning I walked over to ask if and where there was work for the day. Sometimes there was. While working for Mr. Bruno, I helped to lay a floor in the Bank of Montreal at Granville and 10th Avenue, and a big terrazzo floor in the Royal Bank on Granville Street downtown. Of course, as I could not go on with only a part-time job, I looked for other possibilities. The other work I was actually highly qualified for was baking, so I applied to the Four-X Bakery, one of the big bakeries in Vancouver. The person in charge of hiring said, "Yes, we need extra workers for the summer, but you will have to get the OK from the Union." At the Union Headquarters I was told that I would have to be a union member to get the job, but that their union was not taking on new members. I would, however, be allowed to work for two months, in July and August, while most of their members in that bakery were on holiday. Come Labour Day, though, I would lose my job again. So, I started baking again.

The amazing part of the bakery job was that my high qualifications in this trade were unnecessary. This was a bread factory. The prepared dough was in dry form in bags. On the bag was written the amount of water that was to be added. Everything was then put into a big electric dough mixer. After ten or fifteen minutes the dough was taken out, weighed for the loaf size, kneaded, and put in a pan holding four loaves. The pans were loaded on a large trolley rack, ready to go, two pans at the time, into the oven. No bakery skill was required and anybody could do that work.

Because I was only a temporary replacement for other workers, I was given a variety of different posts. One of them was loading the four-bread pans unto the constantly running conveyor belts of the oven – two-at-a-time for eight hours a day, with only two short breaks and a half-hour lunch break. It was very hard work, but I earned fifty-five dollars a week, which was good pay at the time.

As I knew there was no more work for me after Labour Day, and as I did not have any other options in Vancouver, we decided to travel back "home" to Penticton. In those days, the trip meant we had to travel through all the small communities east of Vancouver until we reached Hope, then take the new Hope-Princeton Highway over the mountains. After eight hours of steady traveling, we reached Penticton. Today, the trip takes four-and-a-half hours on the freeway that bypasses all those communities.

When we arrived at the Grundigs', we moved back into our cabin. Home Sweet Home! Again I spent the fall picking fruit, but I also checked to see if I could get a job with a branch of the Four-X Bakery in Penticton. Four-X was in competition with McGavins, another large Vancouver bakery. They both distributed their bread throughout almost all of the province. After the fruit picking was finished at the end of October I presented myself to the manager of the bakery and asked for employment. I was told that as soon as they needed additional help I would be called. They did call me, too – in September 1951. My first job there was making cake doughnuts on a doughnut machine. As before, no skill was needed. I just had to put in the dough powder and watch the machine mix and bake. A little later, I unloaded the ready-baked doughnuts.

During this time Dorothy became pregnant with Marcus. We still lived in the Grundigs' cabin. My work shift was between 4:00 p.m. and midnight. When I drove to work, Dorothy came with me in the car for about two kilometres, then walked home. This gave her her daily exercise. One day in February, just about an hour before I was to leave for work, her water broke and the baby was ready to come into the world. I quickly went to our neighbours, the Clarks, and phoned Doctor John Gibson. He asked me to bring Dorothy to the hospital right away, so on my way to work I dropped her off. Just before my shift at the bakery was over, Dorothy phoned and said, "It's a boy." I visited her on my way home and was happy to find her and the boy in fine condition.

It was the 2nd of February 1952. Winter life in our primitive cabin, without running water or electricity, had been romantic and adventurous for the two of us, but became a bit harder with the baby. My relationship with Dorothy had been intimate. When Marcus was born, Dorothy had to share herself between the two of us. The effect this had on me was noticeable, since I subconsciously felt the urge to be a proper provider. Therefore I worked longer hours, which left less time for us as a twosome. Everyday life became more difficult, and more water was needed. I had to fetch the water from a well, through the snow, and look after the wood stove, for the water needed to be heated to bathe the baby and boiled for washing the diapers. We had to look for better accommodations, and soon. Even though we had an uncertain future ahead of us, I was not concerned. I felt that because we were in Canada I would always find a job, especially since I was prepared and willing to accept any job that came my way.

At that time, we made the acquaintance of the Pruesse family, who had an orchard on the Skaha Lake Benches. On his orchard, Fritz Pruesse had recently built a house for a "steady man." It was unoccupied at that time, and Fritz agreed to rent it to us for a very special rate of twenty dollars a month. That house brought a big change in our lives: now we had electricity and running water, an indoor toilet, and warm rooms – kitchen, living room, two bedrooms, bathroom and an unfinished full basement – although still no telephone. Because there was only one party line in that remote area outside of Penticton, and there were not enough subscriber requests to put in another line, we had to wait. Eventually we did get a phone out there.

The house sat on the edge of the benches, high above the lake, with a spectacular view. From the main road along the lake, a very narrow dirt road led up to the house. At that time the Lakeside Road ended about a mile south of us, at the city limits. In 1959 it was broken through. It now goes all the way to Okanagan Falls.

19. O Sole Mio

While living in the Pruesse house above Skaha Lake and working at the Four-X Bakery, I took a correspondence course from the New York Institute of Photography, which I completed successfully in March 1953. I was very excited about my hobby and converted one bedroom into a darkroom.

From the time I started with serious photography, I believed strongly that I should buy only equipment of the highest quality, even though we had very little money and I couldn't really afford it. For my newly installed darkroom I bought an *Omega* auto-focus enlarger. With that I could handle negatives from 35mm to 4x5 inches. It cost $154 – in 1950 dollars, but more than fifty years later I am still using it. To put the price into perspective, I earned only forty-five dollars a week in the bakery – that enlarger cost almost a month's wages. I also bought a Heiland Electronic Flash Gun, the first one in town. At that time, no professional photographer in town was using one. It was wonderful. No longer did I have to carry a dozen hot flash bulbs in my pockets. The Heiland Electronic Flash Gun has a permanent flash tube powered by a high voltage battery, and can be fired at ten- to twelve-second intervals, which is a big advantage when photographing weddings or other active events.

Of course, while I was setting myself up with the darkroom, I was still working for the bakery. The union – of which I had to be a member in order to work at the bakery – was negotiating for a new contract. Because the union and the management could not come to an agreement, the union held a strike vote. It passed: the majority voted to go on strike. I can't remember how I voted. When the management heard that the workers had voted to strike, they locked us out. For weeks there was no work – and no wages, either. For some reason I still cannot understand, the union had no strike fund. The strike was hard on us, because we could only collect unemployment insurance after a two-week waiting period. The worst thing about the strike, though, was that when labour and management finally came to an agreement and all the staff was hired back on, I wasn't. As I found out later, the management's reason for singling me out was that I had told my colleagues I had worked for the same bakery in Vancouver, doing the same type of work, and got paid fifty-five dollars a week – which was more than we received in Penticton. Because of that, the boss considered me a troublemaker and made sure I did not come back. This put Dorothy and me in a financially difficult situation: I could not pay our rent and I had to rely on the few jobs I could get with my photography.

While I was going through these trials, my landlord, Fritz Pruesse, suggested that I could pay my rent by stuccoing the house in which we lived. Well, since I had worked for the Brown-Byer Plastering Contractors and had seen how they did it, I said, "Yes!" So, without help from anyone, I set about to do what I had never done before: I collected the material for the stucco and to put up a scaffold, and got to work. When I finished, Fritz Pruesse inspected the job. He was satisfied with it, and said to me, "Now you can do my house." I did, too. Thanks to that work, my rent payments were brought up-to-date, and I even had a credit for some months in advance.

One photo job I did during those times of unemployment was especially rewarding. One day, the owner of the Prince Charles Hotel, Mr. Evans Lougheed, came to see me with Roley Ford, a photographer from Vancouver. They had heard of me and wanted me to supply them with some scenic and artistic photographs of Penticton and the surrounding area for a little brochure promoting the city and the hotel. Since I had the kind of photographs they were looking for, they bought them from me, and made the entire brochure with my work. That made me very happy, and helped our finances a little, but I still needed a proper job, and still hoped the bakery would hire me back. It did! In another example of the good luck that has followed me for my whole life, it wasn't long before the bakery manager – the one who had not hired me back after the strike – was fired. The assistant manager, Nels Elder, became manager. One of the first things he did was to come to my house (we still didn't have a phone at that time) to ask me if I wanted my job back at the bakery. Of course I accepted! I was very relieved.

My new job at the bakery was to operate the bread-wrapping machine. To cover up the terrible noise of the machine, sometimes I sang the whole day at the top of my voice. I sang songs of all kinds, everything I knew, and that included some opera arias, and even some German and Italian folk songs. Of course, I wasn't the only one who heard my singing, The other workers heard it plainly, too, although it was all mixed up with the roar of the machine. One day, Jim, a fellow worker, told me that his brother Ralph was going to get married soon. I asked Jim to ask his brother if he would consider hiring me to take his wedding photographs. He said he would ask his brother. The next day Jim told me that the couple had agreed, under the condition that I would sing *Ave Maria* in church at their wedding! In order to get the job, I was bold enough to agree. To practice a little, I asked the piano teacher Mrs. Hendry to coach me. We practiced a few times with the organ at St. Ann's Catholic Church, and with some trepidation I looked forward to my job as photographer and wedding singer.

When the day came and the couple went into the sacristy to sign the register, I put down my camera, slipped up to the balcony where the organ was, and sang Gounaud's *Ave Maria*. After I sang the song, I rushed back down to the sacristy to photograph the couple signing the register, then continued right on with photographing the remaining part of the wedding. This was the only time I ever sang in a church for a wedding. One other time, I sang *O Sole mio!* at a reception for a Japanese wedding, but only because everyone else present – most of them Japanese – had already either recited a poem, told a story, or sang a song. When everyone had performed a piece, the moment came when they all turned their heads and looked at me, the photographer, expecting my contribution. For the sake of good public relations I felt I had no choice but to do something, so I sang, in Italian, the famous Neapolitan song *O Sole mio*. The English translation (not literally) would be something like this:

It's now or never;
come hold me tight.
Kiss me my darling;
be mine tonight.
Tomorrow will be too late:
it's now or never;
my love won't wait!

When I first saw you,
with your smile, so tender,
my heart was captured;
my soul surrendered.
I'd spend a lifetime
waiting for the right time:
now that you're near,
the time is here, at last!

All seemed pleased with the photographer's rather unusual contribution.

Time went on, and on January 4, 1954, Selwyn, our second child, was born. At the same time, Fritz Pruesse told us that we would have to move out of our house, because Bruno and Martha Leipe, the couple he had hired to work in his orchard and for whom the house was actually intended, would soon be moving in. Our growing family had to look for another place to rent. Sadly, every place we looked at was either twice as expensive, half as nice, or half as big as our house at the Pruesses'. When I told this to Fritz Pruesse, he said, "Maybe I can lend you some money, interest free, to make a down payment on a house. You should buy one. You can pay me back as you earn and save some money." This was one of those offers too good to be true, and of course also too good to refuse. Dorothy was excited about the prospect of actually buying a house, but at the same time somewhat apprehensive about how we were going to pay that money back. We discussed the offer briefly, and accepted it almost at once.

Soon enough, Fritz Pruesse lent us $1500, with which we made the down payment on a $5500 house at 464 Caribou Street, near the arena, the schools and my job at the bakery. Fritz had set one condition: he told me that if he needed the money before we paid it back, he would simply borrow it from the bank, but we would pay the interest. This was uniquely generous! Indeed, it happened just like that, too. When Fritz's car broke down soon after that and he needed to buy another one, he had to borrow some money from his bank, and we – happily – paid the interest. Then, in October 1957, Dorothy's mother passed away. From her estate, Dorothy received an inheritance of 10,000 Sfr., which at that time was worth only $2,000. With that money, we were able to pay off the loan from Fritz Pruesse. We were on our own!

After we moved into our house on Caribou Street, I continued to work in the bakery but also offered my photographic services from the house. There too, I converted one bedroom into a darkroom. Even though we now had a telephone, people kept phoning the bakery to speak with me. This was tolerated for a while, until one Friday payday (cash in an envelope), the boss told me, "Hugo, this is your last pay envelope. You are fired." Very taken aback, I asked what I had done wrong. He said, "We get more phone calls for you and your photography than for our bread. Why don't you start your own business?" When I came home and told Dorothy, she also was surprised, and a little concerned as to what would come next. At that time, our monthly financial commitments consisted of paying off the house mortgage at fifty dollars a month, and our car payments of another fifty dollars a month. On my forty-five dollars a week take-home pay we had been able to meet these payments. However, I had no idea how we would meet those obligations now that I no longer had a job. I asked Dorothy if I should look for a new job, any job, or if I should try to earn our income from my photography. She agreed that I should try the photography and see how it worked out. I did, too, confident that I would be able to get more business now that I had all day to look for new photographic jobs. By that time, I had already made a number of portraits of children, adults, groups, and weddings, and my work was slowly getting to be known. I believe it was my artistic touch that caught people's eye. The technical expertise I could learn by reading and practicing all the steps necessary to create technically outstanding photographs, but the artistic balance was the more important part of a successful photograph. I believe I acquired this touch subconsciously by visiting art galleries, especially during my stay in Rome.

For my first wedding job – when I was still living in the Pruesse house and working at the bakery, and long before Jim asked me to sing at his brother's wedding – I was really confident, and really daring, too. Every two weeks I received a booklet on a different topic from the correspondence course of the New York Institute of Photography. After receiving and reading the booklet with the instructions on how to take candid wedding photos and how to get a job photographing a wedding, I followed the instructions: buy a local newspaper, look for wedding announcements, visit the bride and offer your services. That is exactly what I did! The *Penticton Herald* was a weekly paper, issued every Wednesday. I bought a copy at the newspaper office, looked for the wedding announcements, found one, and asked the office staff if they knew the bride. They told me that it was Diane Braidwood, who worked at the Royal Bank. I went straight to the bank, asked for her, introduced myself and offered my services as her wedding photographer for a candid wedding coverage. Logically, she asked to see some wedding photography samples. Since I had never photographed a wedding, I had none to show. I did, however, show her good portraits and scenes, with which I hoped to show my proficiency as a photographer. She liked what she saw, but was not sure, and asked me what I would charge. I did have a business license, even though I worked from my home. For a similar service, established professional photographers in town charged thirty-five dollars, which included twelve 8x10 black and white photographs taken at their studios, in addition to the ones taken at the church. Not to be accused of undercutting the professionals, I quoted fifty dollars for the same number of prints, with the proviso that if they did not like any of the photographs, they could keep all the prints and need not pay for them. I made this offer in order to get the job, and to have samples for my next job, as I quickly saw that I would need those. When the bride heard this "deal," she said she would send her mother to see me and make a decision.

Her mother came to see me in the Pruesse house, with its beautiful view over Skaha Lake. I invited her into our living-dining room and showed her my photographs, the same I had shown to her daughter. At a certain point, I saw her glance under the table at the eight legs that held it up: the table was made out of two sawhorses and a four-by-eight sheet of plywood, covered with a nice white tablecloth! I noticed a faint smile, but she did not let on what she thought, and did not comment on what she had discovered. The truth was that in our first years certain "unnecessary" things like a piano and a radio with a record player were more important to us than some "necessary" things – like a proper table! I repeated my offer to Mrs. Braidwood, and I got the job.

Mrs. Braidwood was a Polish aristocrat, and therefore very cultured. She had high standards, and I knew it would not be easy to please her and to meet her expectations. Following the suggestions from the photo course booklet, I took photographs at the bride's home, at the church and at the reception, including a picture of the throwing of the bouquet just before the newlyweds were going away on their honeymoon. I used my Rolleicord twin lens reflex camera and five rolls of 120-size black and white film of twelve exposures each. From the sixty photos, I selected the twelve best, made 8x10 prints, and put them in an album for a nicely finished presentation. I also showed the balance of the pictures in the form of five 8x10 contact sheets, with twelve 6x6 centimetre prints. To take the photographs I had filled my pockets with three dozen No. 5 flash bulbs, each almost the size of a golf ball. Of course, I had to change the hot flash bulbs after each flash picture. In those days, with each different distance, a photographer had to change the aperture with the help of a guide number based on type of flash bulb and the film speed, too – not an easy feat compared to today's use of automatic, through-the-lens electronic flash exposures and auto-focus zoom lenses. It was after my experience juggling those hot bulbs that I purchased my electronic flash gun.

The wedding was on a Saturday and I had time over the weekend to process the films and make the prints. I took the best print, the couple walking arm in arm out of the church, to the *Penticton Herald* for the Wednesday newspaper; they printed it, with the proper caption and my credit line. After the paper came out, I drove to the parents' house to present my photographs, properly mounted into a wedding album suitable for 8x10 prints. Both parents were at home. Without saying a single word, either of approval or of disapproval, they studied the photographs very carefully. Fortunately for me, while they were still viewing the album, a neighbour, Mrs. Darling (and a darling she turned out to be!), arrived. As soon as she came in, she asked, "How are you? What are you doing?" The bride's parents responded that they were looking at their daughter Diane's wedding pictures. "May I see them, too?" asked Mrs. Darling. And so Mrs. Darling started to leaf through the album. With each additional photograph she saw, she exclaimed how beautiful they were, with many ooohs and aaahs. When she was almost through the album,

Mr. Braidwood disappeared. Moments later, he came back with a small piece of paper in his hand, which was a cheque for $50. He gave it to me with a gracious, "Thank you, Mr. Redivo." Thus I had payment for my first wedding coverage, after which I would be doing many, many more for almost fifty years, without ever having a failure or a dissatisfied client. Until colour photography replaced black and white, I continued with the same system, of showing selected finished prints instead of rough proofs. Later, colour proofs were chosen from 5x5 proof prints presented in suitable proof books. I still made the selection of the best images and recommended them to couples for their albums; by choosing from the proofs couples could fill out their albums with different or additional images. As the years went by, those albums became priceless heirlooms for those couples. I went on to photograph their babies and later also the weddings of some of those babies.

20. I May be Crazy

For about a year I operated my photography business from our home on Caribou Street, and made enough money to meet our mortgage and car payments, and just enough to barely feed and cloth the family of four. During that time, I met Bob Morrison, who was a reporter and photographer at the *Penticton Herald*. We talked about photography and how we could improve our lot. One day he came to me and told me that the Cameo Studio was for sale for $7500 and that we should try to buy it. I just laughed, because I had no money, only debts, and he had only a small salary. Neither of us had any assets on which we could borrow money, either. In conversation with my friend Fritz Pruesse, I casually mentioned that we had the chance of buying a studio – if only we had the money. He told me that if he had had the money, he would have lent it to us. Then he suggested we talk to Mr. Oscar Matson, who at that time was the Mayor of Penticton, and who was known to lend money for risky deals, but would add ten percent of the amount to be paid back. Asking doesn't cost anything, and we had nothing to lose, so Bob Morrison and I went to Mr. Matson to ask him for a loan of $7500 to buy the business from the vendor, Mr. Harry Davies. The Cameo Studio was a camera shop and photo studio that also sold art supplies and offered a picture framing service. Mr. Matson asked us if we had any collateral. When we told him we didn't, he was reluctant to continue the conversation. However, because he knew me from when I had taken photographs of him and his wife Margaret (now at the time of this writing ninety-nine years old) when they were leaving for Germany to see the Penticton Vees win the World Hockey Championship against Russia, he said he would consider our request and would talk to Mr. Davies about the business and ask him if he thought we could handle it and run it successfully. He closed our meeting by telling us to come back the next day. Since Harry Davies was anxious to sell, he convinced Mr. Matson that the business was sound and argued that since we were both young we could easily run it even better than he had. When we returned the next day, Mr. Matson said, "I may be crazy, but I will give you the money. You need $7500, but you have to sign an I.O.U.

for $8250, to be payable at the current interest rate of 6%, with monthly pay-
ments of $300." Looking at these numbers was scary; we could have done it,
but since there would not have been much left for salary to take home every
month, we bargained for a $200 monthly payment. Mr. Matson agreed.

On August 15, 1955, Hugo Redivo and Bob Morrison took possession of
the Cameo Studio. It was mid-week: on the upcoming Saturday I had to photograph a wedding, on location in the candid style, as I had done so many
times, but also in the studio, which was a first for me. I had never used a 5x7
studio camera, nor handled studio lights, but I managed it all without any
difficulty. Developing the 5x7 sheet film, which I also did for the first time,
did not go so well, however: the darkroom was such a narrow and crowded
area that the processing tanks were too close together. In the complete dark-
ness necessary to process panchromatic black and white film, it was difficult
to distinguish which solution was which. By mistake, I put all the 5x7 sheet
films, in hangers, into the fixer, whereas they should have first gone into the
developer. As soon as I discovered, by touch, that there was another tank to
the left of the fixer tank, I transferred the films. Unfortunately, I did not rinse
them in water first. The films developed anyway, but not to a level that high
quality prints could be made from those negatives. I could only salvage some
of the images of the groups and the bridal couple, but because I had a complete set of candid wedding photographs, the damage was not too great. After
that experience I took corrective steps to prevent the same mistake ever happening again.

This first year was a big learning experience. For some reason, I took on
all the selling of cameras and art supplies, and all the picture framing, too.
For the first few months, the framing workshop was in Mr. Davies' basement.
After that, we moved it to our neighbour, Mr. Niederman's, basement, and,
still later, into an old, drafty, unheated garage behind the store. During that
first year, not only did I do all the selling in the store, but I had to keep track of
the inventory and do the ordering as well. Since Bob Morrison had kept his
contract with the *Penticton Herald* – to be on call and to supply them with news
photographs – he was mostly out of the store. I also had to do most of the
studio portraits, in addition to the weddings, because most of the time people

asked for me by name, and because Bob just was not on the premises very often. When he was, he was often invited out to coffee by business friends, which he considered necessary public relations.

After an accountant had set up our initial books, Bob Morrison took over the bookkeeping. Every month, we paid off $200 on our loan, and each of us took a salary of $200. This was equivalent to my wages in the bakery. We managed to get by. In addition, Dorothy earned some extra money by retouching and spotting negatives and photographs I brought home for her to work on, but because the main load of the business was on my shoulders I put in very long hours. Store hours were from 9:00 am to 5:30 pm, Saturdays until 9:00 pm. The store was closed on Wednesday afternoons so I could work undisturbed in the darkroom. During the week, however, I burned the midnight oil, and either had to work in the darkroom or write orders to keep the inventory up to date, often until midnight.

When Bob Morrison and I entered into our partnership, we had agreed to try for one year and then reassess our situation. Because I had done so much work in that year, I longed to get out. As the business had paid off $2400 during that year, I asked for $1200, my half of what was paid off. Bob agreed and tried to raise the money, but he could not get the money, neither from the bank nor from any relatives he approached. After that, he agreed that I could buy *him* out, but for $1500, not $1200. When I went to the Bank of Montreal and asked if I could borrow this money on top of the money we then still owed, the manager, a Mr. Walton – actually the brother of the famous British composer – asked me, "Can you handle it?"

"Certainly," I replied. "I did it more or less alone for a full year already!" At that, Mr. Walton opened his desk drawer, pulled out a piece of paper, wrote $1500 on it, and said, "OK, sign here and pay out Bob Morrison," which I did. From then on, I did all the work and ran the store by myself. Dorothy did the retouching, spotting, and bookkeeping. We had a better salary and could afford some extras.

Three-and-a-half years went by quickly, and the business was paid off. For some time, we had been saying we would go to Europe "next year," but "next year" never came. Finally, we promised ourselves to go once the business was paid off. That date was May 10, 1959 – exactly ten years to the day after we were admitted to Canada and received the landed immigrant stamp in our passports. Another reason to travel in early May was because our daughter Rhea, who was born on May 25, 1958, was under one year old and her air fare was only $10, instead of half the adult rate. At that time, the adult fare for the trip from Vancouver to Paris, via Toronto and New York, was $710. The two boys were half that. Our total fare for the trip amounted to $2140. At that time this would have been enough to pay one-third down on a house. We also had to budget for some spending money, but since the exchange rate was very favourable for us, at four Swiss Francs to the dollar, this was not a great hardship. The few times we used a hotel room, for example, we paid twelve Swiss Francs, or three dollars.

To make the trip, I had to go back to the bank again to borrow money. I asked for $3600, to be paid back after we returned. The bank manager was reluctant to lend us the money for a trip to Europe in 1959, but when I explained that my father and Dorothy's mother had both died since we left them ten years earlier, and that we wanted to see the two remaining parents once more, and that they had never seen our three children, he relented and gave us the money on compassionate grounds. Thinking back, it was rather daring to undertake such a travel project with three children aged seven, five and one, at such a price, and all with borrowed money, but we never regretted it.

"What will you do with the business, though?" the bank manager asked.

I explained that a few months earlier I had hired an Englishman, Mr. Michael Burn, who appeared to be trustworthy enough, and that I would put him in charge. After the loan was approved, I then hired a photographer from Vancouver, and engaged a local student, Bill Stockand. In addition, I relied on a chartered accountant to keep an eye on all money transactions and to co-sign cheques and any other items that required signatures. My instructions were, "Do the best you can. You don't need to write me when things go wrong; I will find out soon enough when I come back!" In the back of my mind, I was thinking that if I came back to find that everything was gone, I could just start all over again, which was possible in Canada at that time. I believed that if my employees made enough money to pay their wages and didn't get me in debt with excessive stock purchases, it would be all right. And that is what happened.

It is a good thing I told them not to phone me, though, because the photographer would have alarmed me greatly. He was simply unreliable. He certainly appeared to be a pleasant person, even drove us to the Vancouver Airport to send us off, and we left him with our Chevrolet sedan to use to go to weddings or other outside jobs. When we came back, however, we discovered he had put on three thousand miles during that time, driving all over the Northwest, including trips to Seattle and Edmonton. When I learned of his conduct, I had to terminate his employment. The result was that he threatened me by walking on the other side of the street past the store, carrying a rifle. I think we called the police, and I believe he then left town. I recall hearing on the radio later, during the Winter Olympics in Innsbrück, that a Canadian photographer with his name was arrested for misconduct.

21. *Home*

For the three-and-a-half months we were in Europe, we rented a French Simca car in Paris. The deal was that after that rental period we could either bring the car back or pay the money for the balance of the price of the car. Because we were foreigners, the final price of the car was without taxes, which made it considerably cheaper than the regular market price, especially in Switzerland. As a result, we were able to sell the car in Switzerland for a price that included our rental fee, which meant we had use of this new car for three-and-a-half months practically without cost.

On our way to Europe, we had a lucky break at the La Guardia Airport in New York. We were supposed to board a Pan Am four-engine propeller plane to Paris, but this plane was overbooked. Fortunately, Pan Am made another plane available to fly to Paris. This second plane was almost empty, and all the passengers had plenty of room to stretch and sleep, which was especially good for the two boys. We arrived the next morning, reasonably rested after the almost twelve-hour flight – except for Dorothy, who had nursed and looked after the one-year-old Rhea, who had not slept well in the small bassinet provided by the airline.

In Paris we went to the car rental office in a side street off the Champs Elysées to collect our car. Even though I was polite and spoke a passable French, I was practically ignored, and was told to come back the next day. We spent the day seeing the most obvious sights of the city, like the Eiffel Tower and Notre Dame. The next day, full of hope again, we returned to the car rental office, but once again I was ignored and made to wait. That's when I used the "rude American" tactic. I started screaming, in English, that I had paid for my rental car, that I was told it would be ready, and here I was waiting, for the second day, with a family, with three small children, and being just ignored, and that I wanted my car right now! Many people in the offices and the waiting room heard the commotion that I created. In the shortest of time, I had my papers and the keys for the car. Someone accompanied us downstairs to street level where my car was sitting, ready to be driven away. I started the car and drove out on the Champs Elysées with its six unmarked lanes of traffic in each direction. Each driver was driving where there was a hole in the traffic pattern and trying hard neither to hit anybody nor to be hit. Finding myself suddenly in this unruly and unaccustomed flow of traffic, I had to get back into a side street again and catch my breath. After watching the traffic whiz by for a short while, with my family in the car quite quiet, I decided, *when in Paris, do as the Parisians do*, and drove right out into the traffic again, honking my horn when necessary, as all the others did. In the end, I navigated quite well through it all. It was the same throughout Europe: on the German Autobahn, with its unrestricted speeds; in Italy, where cars are not driven by the rules of the road but rather by hit and miss; in Spain; and in the South of France. I did not have any problems for the whole three-and-a-half months.

We made our headquarters in Hombrechtikon, near Zurich, where Dorothy's father, Fritz Vögeli, lived with his second wife, Hedy Höhn. From there we made all our various trips. Sometimes we left the children with Dädda and Hedi, sometimes we took all three along, sometimes only the boys, and once we left the boys in a children's home in Siegriswil.

Our first trip was with the whole family to my home in Dalheim, to visit my mother and my brother Bruno and his children. To see my mother again after ten years was an emotional encounter for both of us. She was overjoyed to get to see our children. It was particularly rewarding to her to be able to speak with them, which she could, since we had spoken German with them as they grew up. My brother Bruno and family lived with her in our house. To help look after our mother, I bequeathed my half of the future inheritance of our house to my brother. The German economy was improving and the beginning of the *Wirtschaftswunder* could be felt.

Our second trip – this one without the children – was to Spain. At that time, it was a popular, inexpensive tourist destination, untouched by World War II. With us on the two-week trip to Spain were Dorothy's sister Elisabeth and her fourteen-year-old daughter, Liselotte. In Spain, the four of us stayed in Tossa de Mar at the Costa Brava, made excursions by boat to other nearby fishing villages, and visited Barcelona, where we saw the famous art gallery, the Museum Nacional d'Art de Catalunya, which houses paintings by most of

THE AUTOBIOGRAPHY OF HUGO REDIVO

the important Spanish and European Painters. We saw the Santa Maria – the ship Columbus sailed across the Atlantic to discover America, and the former World Exhibition site, too. The Santa Maria did not look big enough to cross unchartered waters in the hope of reaching a destination in the east by sailing west! We found all of the quarters on the ship very small. Seeing it there, Dorothy and I both thought that if we had emigrated a hundred years earlier we would have crossed – and would have been tossed around in – the Atlantic in a ship much like it. There were no obvious signs of Franco's rule, except the large number of police, the *Guardia Civil*. We saw them everywhere, even inside night clubs. When we were visiting the site of the former World Exhibition, we came to a large hall where refugees, perhaps still from the Spanish Civil War, were housed in small cubicles, separated only by large blankets. Once, we were almost arrested. Elisabeth and Dorothy were tired, so they stretched out on benches in the park. Liselotte and I were wandering about and suddenly saw the *Guardia Civil* talking to them, so we rushed over and proved to the police that we were together and legitimate tourists from Switzerland and Canada, not loiterers. After they checked our passports, they let us go.

Another trip was with the boys to Nice and to the Ile du Levant. The Ile du Levant is one of the Iles d'Hydres, southeast of Toulon and southwest of St. Tropez. To reach it, you embark in the port of Le Lavender, between Toulon and St. Tropez, and sail directly south. The island is divided by a mountain range – the military occupies one side and a nudist colony the other. When not lying on the rocky beach to sunbathe or to swim in the ocean in the buff, the dress code for going into the village, or to and from the hotel, was the "minimum," a tiny triangle to fit over one's private parts. I recall a funny incident, when two Italian young men arrived at the beach. One of them wondered out loud if he should take off his trunks. The other encouraged him to do so. In the end, the first young man did decide to take off his bathing suit, but to do so he went behind a big rock, so that nobody could see him, then he came out from behind the rock carrying his trunks.

Whatever I saw in all the countries we visited convinced me that I had made the right move to go to Canada. Wherever I encountered relatives, friends and casual acquaintances, I sensed a degree of envy. They could not believe that in 1959, after only ten years in Canada, poor Hugo could afford to make a three-month-long trip to Europe, with a family of three children.

We stopped in Monte Carlo to see the famous Museum of Oceanography, with its displays of huge skeletons of whales and other sea creatures. As it was in the middle of summer, at the height of tourist season, we could not find suitable or reasonably priced accommodations for the four of us. We slept on the gravelly beach instead. Another time, when we left the boys in the *Kinderheim Paradiesli* (Little Paradise Daycare), we went to Roveredo in Piano. On that same trip we visited Murano, Venezia and Padua. Murano is one of a group of islands in the Lagoon of Venice, and is famous for its glass artisans. The art of glass blowing dates back to the eighth century there, but was interrupted for five hundred years, starting in the fourteenth century and ending in the middle of the nineteenth century. In Venice itself we enjoyed travelling in a gondola on the canals under a shining moon with a gondolier singing to us. It was a very romantic experience. In Padua we visited the Duomo di Sant'Antonio and saw all the "thank you" tokens from people who had been healed by the saint after praying to him and making vows. These tokens included crutches, canes, and many written notes. On our return, we made various excursions within Switzerland. We drove over most of the Alpine passes, and visited many remote areas. The time went by quickly, and on Labour Day in September we were back home.

I took thirty-four thirty-six-exposure rolls of Kodachrome ASA 10 slide film with me to Europe, as well as my new Leica M-3 Rangefinder camera. For the fall season of Adult Education courses after I got back to Penticton, I offered four sessions of slide presentations entitled "With Hugo Redivo and his Colour Camera through Europe." About twenty-five to thirty people came for each of the four nights. By pacing the showings properly, I was able to show three hundred slides per night without boring my audience.

Because our Europe trip was so satisfying and fulfilling, we did not regret leaving Europe and our relatives behind us a second time, since we now knew that it would be possible to come back again another time for a visit. We were not homesick at all – in fact, we were looking forward to being back home in Canada. I was anxious to see the condition of my business, and without any regrets for having made the journey with my family, was prepared to accept whatever condition I would find. As it turned out, although the business had not made any money for me to draw from, it had supported itself and had paid all the wages to three employees. What's more, the inventory was not depleted.

Of course, the flight home was much quicker than the leisurely ocean voyage of 1949. We were happy the trip took a day-and–a-half instead of a week-and-a-half. After our return from Europe, we happily settled back into our daily Canadian routine. The children started their school year, and Dorothy continued to look after them, and me, besides doing all the spotting and retouching. I got ready to order Christmas stock for the store and to render my photographic services to the community. Portraits and weddings were the stable income, as I settled, just like Axel Munthe so many years earlier in Anacapri, into my own little piece of paradise, completely refreshed, mentally and physically, after the return from Europe, and ready to fully dedicate myself again to my work, especially because the business had not suffered from my long absence.

The assumption that a normal, familiar routine of work and daily life would continue was altered one Wednesday in 1960, however, by a fateful phone call from Dorothy, when she interrupted my routine work in the darkroom, asking me to come with her and a real estate agent to look at a building lot on Skaha Lake. I was rather annoyed to be interrupted in my one free day of darkroom work, because I knew we could never afford to buy a building lot on Skaha Lake, but I went anyway. However, we did buy the lot, and we did build our own Villa San Michele on it. We called it Casa Miralago, and moved into it in May 1961. We still live in it. Franca, our fourth child, was born that June. We were home, together.